WHAT
GOD
WANTS

WHAT
GOD
WANTS

A Compelling Answer to
Humanity's Biggest Question

NEALE DONALD WALSCH

ATRIA BOOKS
NEW YORK LONDON TORONTO SYDNEY

ATRIA BOOKS

1230 Avenue of the Americas
New York, NY 10020

Library of Congress Cataloging-in-Publication Data

Walsch, Neale Donald.
    What God wants: a compelling answer to humanity's biggest
question / by Neale Donald Walsch.
        p. cm.
    1. God—Miscellanea. 2. Spiritual life—Miscellanea. I. Title.

BF1999.W2289 2005
04—dc22

2004062687

ISBN-13: 978-0-7432-6713-7
ISBN-10:   0-7432-6713-3
ISBN-13: 978-0-7432-6714-4 (Pbk)
ISBN-10:   0-7432-6714-1 (Pbk)

This Atria Books trade paperback edition January 2006

10 9 8 7 6 5 4 3 2 1

ATRIA BOOKS is a trademark of Simon & Schuster, Inc.

Manufactured in the United States of America

For information regarding special discounts for bulk purchases,
please contact Simon & Schuster Special Sales at 1-800-456-6798 or
business@simonandschuster.com.

WHAT
GOD
WANTS

1.

Very few people will be able to believe what's in this book.

At least, at first.

That may make it one of the most unbelievable books of all time.

2.

This book answers the most important question in human history.

What does God want?

For many people that answer will be startling.

Even for those who aren't completely surprised, the answer will be dramatically different. It will not even come close to the ideas that people usually hear about God.

Humanity's ideas about God produce humanity's ideas about life and about people. Dramatically *different* ideas about God will produce dramatically *different* ideas about life and about people. If the world could use anything right now, that's it.

We stand today on the brink of a global cultural war. The opening volleys have already been exchanged. The really major clashes, the unthinkable Future World battles, may be yet to come.

Given the direction in which humanity appears to be moving, it may seem as though this larger conflict is inevitable. It isn't. There's something very powerful that can stop it: *dramatically different ideas about God and dramatically different ideas about life and about people.*

Such ideas, if accepted and adopted, will produce dramatically different ways of living and being. Values will change. Priorities will change. Power structures and power *holders* will change.

Some of those power holders do not want any of this to happen.

That may make this not only one of the most un-believable books of all time, but also one of the most dangerous.

3.

How long has it been since you've read a dangerous book?

You'll be in and out of this one in very little time. It's a short book. So it's not only dangerous, it's fast.

Fast and dangerous. That's often a fascinating combination. Maybe even a little exciting. Danger and excitement are two sides of the same coin. Which of the two you experience depends on whether you're racing *toward* something or *away* from it.

Which way are you racing with regard to change? Do you want things to remain pretty much the same, or do you want things to be different?

If you want things to stay the way they are, you could find this book dangerous. If you can't wait for things to change, you could find it exciting. Which do you want?

"Well," you might say, "that depends on what we're talking about here. Are we talking about my life? My job? My marriage? My relationship? My health? Or are we talking about my country? The world at large? The international political scene? The global challenges being faced by humanity?"

So let me help you with that. We're talking about all of it. Every bit of it. Not one thing or the other, but all of it. Because the information in this book could *change* all of it.

Change can be a dangerous thing to suggest, not only around people of power (to whom change is the ultimate threat) but also around ordinary people (for whom change is threatening simply because it leads to the unknown).

Former U.S. vice president Al Gore had it exactly right in a September 2004 interview in the *New Yorker*:

"In a world of disconcerting change, when large and complex forces threaten familiar and comfortable guideposts, the natural impulse is to grab hold of the tree trunk that seems to have the deepest roots and hold on for dear life and *never question the possibility that it's not going to be the source of your salvation.*"

The final part of that sentence (italics mine) tells the tale of humanity's belief about God and life in fifteen words. Mr. Gore confirms this with his next statement. "And the deepest roots," he says, "are in philosophical and religious traditions that go way back."

Al Gore's insight leaves us all facing a thunderous question: Is the *way forward* to be found by going *way back?*

The answer is no.

And while, as the former vice president notes, we never question the possibility that our philosophical and religious traditions are not going to be the source of our salvation—presumably because we feel threatened by such questioning—could there be times when *not* to question those traditions presents an even larger threat?

The answer is yes. *And this is one of those times.*

The biggest danger in the world today is not the asking of questions but the assumption that we have all the answers; not the invitation to change but the tendency to run from change; not dramatically new ideas about God and about Life but the same old ideas.

If some of those old ideas continue to be embraced, life as the human race now knows it may not survive the first half of the twenty-first century. The way things are going, it may not even survive the first quarter.

I know, I know, that sounds like an exaggeration.

It's not.

Pick up the morning paper. Turn on CNN.

In the years immediately ahead the human race could make a dramatic upward jump in its evolutionary process, or it could fall back, staggering and stumbling and ultimately crumbling under the weight of its own past misunderstandings.

It's happened before.

It is what can occur when the technological advancement of a species races ahead of its moral, ethical, and spiritual development. Then what the universe has to deal with is children playing with matches.

These days, that's us.

The human race is in the childhood of its evolution. There's nothing wrong with that. Childhood can be a wonderful time. But it's also a time when great care must be taken.

If we watch what we are doing during our childhood—if, as author Robert Fulghum suggests, we look both ways before crossing, if we learn to share, if we hold hands and keep track of each other, if we walk and don't run, if we quit pushing and say we're sorry when we do, if we clean up our messes, and if we stop fighting with our brothers and sisters—we'll get to grow up, and our future can be spectacular.

I believe that's what will happen. I believe the future we're about to create is going to be so spectacular! But I also know it could turn out another way. And I know that if we don't start behaving, it very well might. Failure to acknowledge this is foolhardy. It's more than foolhardy. It's irresponsible. It's what a child would do.

Most people want to believe that humanity is indestructible, that our species cannot be eradicated or eliminated or negatively impacted in any truly widespread or nonreversible way by anyone or anything.

In view of recent world events, this seems to suggest that most people are willing to believe the unbelievable. And that brings up an interesting question. If people are willing to believe the unbelievable, *why not believe what's in this book?*

4.

Many people will simply be *afraid* to believe what's in this book.

A dramatically different idea is going to be presented here just 12,108 words from now. So opposed to this idea is the established order that, in some countries, if you said aloud the things that are in this book, you could be killed.

Not by an angry mob.

By the government.

You could be accused of committing a crime against the laws of the land, and sentenced to death. In other countries, while you might not be killed, you could be criticized, vilified, and ostracized. You could also be removed from any place of influence you might hold, and your views would almost certainly be marginalized.

Yes, that's how dangerous what is written here is.

Clearly, *What God Wants* is not unimportant information. It's so important, in fact, that the words are presented in initial caps and italic type wherever the term is used throughout this book. I wanted those words to stand out, so that they make a point in and of themselves.

You see, millions of people all over the world have been living their lives based on the information they have been given about *What God Wants,* and if the world's prior information on this topic is inaccurate, the world could be in big trouble.

5.

The world's prior information on this topic is inaccurate.

The world is in big trouble.

6.

The world does not have to be in big trouble. It is because it chooses to be. Its people could make a different choice.

I think that very soon they will. I think people have had enough. They've had enough of the violence and the terror and the killing. They've had enough of the bickering and the quarreling and the fighting that leads to it.

They've had enough of their own lives not working, of seeing their own relationships falling apart, of watching their own careers crumble, of having their own dreams dissolve and disappear.

They've had enough of everything being such a struggle in our world, with every day filling itself with adversity and difficulty all over the globe. They've had enough of human society taking two steps forward and one step back, constantly, constantly, constantly trudging into the wind.

The human race is losing patience with itself. I think

people are saying, "There's *got* to be another way." We're becoming more and more clear that there is. We simply have to make that choice.

Sometimes people think they *must* live the way they are living because they *have* no choice. The appearance of things can often make it look as though this is very, very real. But it is never real. Never.

People *do* have a choice, and this book is going to prove that to you. People have a choice in the life they are creating, and they have a choice in how they are experiencing the life they are now living. Before you get to the final page here, you're going to be given the most powerful tool there is with which to make your choices real. For now, know this: People who make a different choice are people who make a different world.

It is time now for the Choice Makers to step forward. If they do not, the world will continue moving in the direction in which it is moving. That is not a direction in which humanity says it wishes to go. Yet what is humanity willing to do about that? This is the question now before the world.

If humanity's highest idea about the direction that it wishes to take is not asserted now, its lowest idea could be embraced by default. That is what is happening at this moment in some people's minds in many parts of the world.

There are those who say that this is how it is because this is how it *has to be*. These are, they say, the End Times—and this is *What God Wants*.

Yet people *can* be saved, they say. People do not have to be Left Behind. When the Tribulation is at hand, people can be saved. All they have to do is finally accept the Good News.

Well, have I got good news for you.

Humanity does not understand *What God Wants*.

7.

Consider this: If humanity *does* understand *What God Wants,* and if the present world situation is the best that humanity can do after all these years with that information, how much hope can there be for a brighter tomorrow?

If we really know everything that it is truly important to know about God—and if all that has been revealed, all that has been taught, all that has been said and sung, about God has brought humanity to *this,* then what good has all of it been?

Yet if there is something *new* for us to learn, something *more* for us to understand about God, then it's still possible for the human condition to change. Hope returns. Not hope for something better in the Hereafter, when life as we've known it on the earth has been destroyed, but hope for something better right here right now, *before* everything has been destroyed.

That hope cannot be realized, however, until some very important questions are asked and answered.

Is it true that humanity is utterly stubborn, completely unwilling and absolutely unable to overcome its most primitive instincts? *Or is it possible that there is still some teaching left to be done, some data still missing, some important aspect of God and Life still not understood?*

Could it be that the problem is not with the receivers of the information, but with the information itself?

Could it be that humanity's understanding of God and of Life is not so much "wrong" as it is simply incomplete?

Finally, is it time for humanity to throw open the door of inquiry about God in a new way?

For far too long the world's discussion about God has been moving in only one direction, led in the main by those who say that we understand all there is that's really important for us to understand about God, and who assert that humanity's problems are not caused by human beings who fail to understand, but by human beings who fail to *act* on their understanding.

This is a popular notion, but it's a misconception. Just the opposite has been true. It has been people who *did* act on what they understood about God who have caused many of our biggest problems.

These are people who thought they knew *What God Wants.*

It's people who thought they knew *What God Wants* who created the 200 years of the Christian Crusades and the horrors of the Inquisition, seeking to win the world for Christianity.

It's people who thought they knew *What God Wants* who told armies of Muslims to send marauders far and wide to conquer every land and culture and bring it under the Nation of Islam.

It's people who thought they knew *What God Wants* who called themselves the Chosen People and reclaimed land they declared to be originally their own, ignoring the fact that history had caused it to be inhabited for thousands of years by others, and telling those others to now leave portions of that land, and to live where and how they are told to live, as second-class citizens without equal rights in their own home.

It's people who thought they knew *What God Wants* who hanged men and women in town squares, and burned others at the stake, holding up the Good Book and declaring them to be witches.

It's people who thought they knew *What God Wants* who passed laws making it illegal for humans of differing races to marry, or for consenting adults to engage in certain sexual practices.

It's people who thought they knew *What God Wants* who created cultural prohibitions forbidding people to sing or dance, draw pictures of any person, or play music of any kind except sacred songs.

It's people who thought they knew *What God Wants* who said that it was not okay to even utter or write the name of G-D—but that it *was* okay to kill in G-D's name.

Is all of this really *What God Wants?*

Are you sure?

It is important to be sure, because we're not talking about a small thing here.

There is much that we have been taught about *What God Wants.* Are these teachings accurate? Let's take a look.

8.

Here is a quick survey of some of the things many people have been told by their ancestors, by their parents, by their teachers, and by other authority figures in their lives about *What God Wants*. It may be tough for some of you to get through this survey. Please do it anyway.

These passed-on messages have created the here-and-now views, ideas, and experiences of millions of people who at least loosely adhere to, or live in cultures that have been deeply affected by, the doctrines of Judaism, Christianity, and Islam, the big three of the world's organized religions. Some of these teachings also became a part of other religions. The result of this is that a huge portion of the world's people have been exposed to these ideas and deeply affected by them.

Let's take the most obvious topics first.

God

Many humans have been told that *What God Wants* is for humans to understand that God is the Supreme Being, the Creator of Heaven and Earth, the Giver of Life, Omnipotent, Omniscient, Omnipresent, and Wise Beyond Human Understanding.

God is the Alpha and the Omega, the beginning and the end, the Unmoved Mover, separate from humanity, but the creator of it in His own image. Separate from life, but the Creator of it, as His gift to humanity.

Most humans have been told that God is a single God, a unified God, the Only God there is. *Allah* means, literally, "the God." Some humans have been told that this One God is divided into Three Parts, one of which became human. Some humans have been told that there is more than one God. And some humans have been told that there is no God at all. The majority of humans in the twenty-first century believe in a God of some sort.

Most of those who do believe in God have been told that *What God Wants* is Love and Justice.

To fulfill the first mandate, God has granted each human being ample and repeated opportunity to be reconciled with Him.

To fulfill the second mandate, God, at the end of each human life, sits in Judgment of every human soul, deciding at this Reckoning whether the soul has earned ever-lasting reward in Heaven or everlasting damnation in Hell.

Most humans have been told that God is a jealous God, God is a vengeful God, God is an angry God who can be filled with wrath and who uses violence directly on human beings—and who invites and even commands human beings to do so on each other.

They've also been told that God is a caring God, a compassionate God, a merciful God, a loving God who wants nothing but the best for human beings. All that humans have to do is obey Him.

It's easy for humans to know how to obey God because God has told humans exactly what to do and what not to do. It's all there in Sacred Scripture. It can be found also in the words and in the teaching of God's personal representative on earth.

These are the beliefs of much of humanity.

One result of this teaching: Many human beings are afraid of God. They also love God. So, many humans confuse fear and love, seeing them as connected in some way. Where God is concerned, we love to be afraid (we have made it a *virtue* to be "God fearing"), and we are afraid not to love (we are commanded to "Love the Lord thy God with all thy mind, all thy heart, and all thy soul").

Humans fear what God will do to them if they do not

obey Him. They have been told He will punish them with everlasting torment. Many human beings therefore rely heavily on their understanding of God's word and God's desires and what meets God's approval when regulating their lives, interpreting situations or events, and making decisions.

When U.S. president George W. Bush was asked if he ever sought the advice of his father, the first President Bush, he replied that he sought counsel from "a higher Father."

The day after his re-election in November 2004, Bush was sent a letter by Bob Jones III, president of the fundamentalist college that bears his name, in which he was told that he should use his electoral mandate to appoint conservative judges and approve legislation "defined by biblical norm."

"In your re-election, God has graciously granted America—though she doesn't deserve it—a reprieve from the agenda of paganism," Jones wrote Bush in a congratulatory letter posted on the university's Web site November 3, 2004.

"You have been given a mandate. . . . Put your agenda on the front burner and let it boil. You owe the liberals nothing. They despise you because they despise your Christ," the letter said.

When the then-new spiritual leader of Hamas, Abdel Aziz Rantisi, delivered a speech at Gaza's Islamic University in March 2004, he told those assembled that "God declared war" against America, Bush, and Israeli prime minister Ariel Sharon. Rantisi added, "The war of God continues against them and I can see the victory coming up from the land of Palestine by the hand of Hamas." Two weeks later Rantisi was dead, killed by an Israeli rocket attack on his car.

Earlier it was said, "Humanity's ideas about God produce humanity's ideas about life and about people."

This is painfully clear. This is painfully obvious.

God's Word and God's Messenger

Many humans have been told that *What God Wants* is for God's Word to be recognized as being contained in the Holy Scriptures and Sacred Texts, and for God's Messenger to be honored and listened to and followed.

There are many Holy Scriptures and Sacred Texts, including the Adi Granth, the Bhagavad Gita, the Book of Mormon, the Hadith, the I Ching, the Kojiki, the Lun-yü, the Mahabharata, the Mathnawi, the New Testament, the Pali Canon, the Qur'an, the Talmud, the Tao Te

Ching, the Torah, the Upanishads, the Vedas, and the Yoga Sutras, to name a few. Many humans have been told that only one of these texts is the right one. The rest are wrong. If you choose the teachings of the "wrong" one, you'll go to Hell.

There are many Messengers, including Noah, Abraham, Moses, Confucius, Siddhārtha Gautama (who has been called the Buddha), Jesus of Nazareth (who has been called the Savior), Muhammad (who has been called the Greatest Prophet), Patanjai (who has been called the Enlightened One), Baha'u'llah (who has been called the Blessed One), Jalal al-Din Rumi (who has been called the Mystic), Paramahansa Yogananda (who has been called the Master), Joseph Smith (who has been called many things), and others. Many humans have been told that only one of these messengers is the right one. The rest are wrong. If you choose the message of the "wrong" one, you'll go to Hell.

One result of this teaching: Human beings have been trying to figure out which is the right text and who is the right messenger for thousands of years. The followers of certain messengers and the believers in certain texts have sought to convince the rest of the world that the messenger and text of their persuasion is the only one to which people should turn.

On many occasions throughout history these attempts at conversion have turned violent. There has scarcely been a day on this planet when a battle has not been fought or a human being not killed in the name of God, or for God's Cause.

The Holy Scriptures of all major religions indicate that vanquishing, punishing, and killing is something that God Himself has repeatedly done, and so vanquishing, punishing, and killing in God's name and in the name of God's Messenger is acceptable and, in some circumstances, required.

This is, many of the world's people believe, *What God Wants*.

Heaven and Hell

Many humans have been told that *What God Wants* is for people to live good lives, and for good people to go to Heaven or Paradise after their deaths, while bad people go to Hell, Gehenna, or Hades. Those in Heaven will live in unending bliss in reunion with God, and those in Hell will live with other evildoers who have been damned to eternal torture. Where each individual soul goes will be decided at the Reckoning on Judgment Day.

Some humans have been told that Hell is a temporary experience during which sinners are tormented by demons until the debt created by the evil of their lives has been paid, while others have been informed that Hell is but a phase in a soul's journey as it passes through many experiences of reincarnation.

One result of this teaching: Millions of people have structured their entire lives around the struggle to avoid "going to Hell" and around the hope of "getting to Heaven." They have done extraordinary and sometimes shocking things to produce this outcome.

The concept of Heaven and Hell has shaped not only their behavior, but their entire understanding of life itself. It has also shaped human history.

Life

Many humans have been told that *What God Wants* is for life to be a school, a place of learning, a time of testing, a brief and precious opportunity to migrate the soul back to Heaven, back to God, whence it came.

Many humans have also been told that it's when life ends that the real joy begins. All of life should be considered a prelude, a forerunner, a platform upon which is built the soul's experience of eternity. Life should therefore be led with an eye toward the Afterlife, for what is earned now will be experienced forever.

Most humans also believe that *What God Wants* is for people to understand that life consists of what people can see, hear, taste, touch, and smell—and nothing more.

One result of this teaching: Humans believe that life is not easy, nor is it supposed to be. It's a constant struggle. In this struggle, anything other than what is perceived by the five senses is considered "supernatural" or "occult" and falls, therefore, into the category of "trafficking with the Devil" and "the work of Satan."

Humans are struggling to get back to God, and into God's good graces. They are struggling to get back home. This is what life is about. It's about the struggle of the soul, living within the body, to get back home, to return to God, from Whom it has been separated.

Most people of religious persuasion focus heavily on Heaven and Hell. Those who believe that "getting to Heaven" is the ultimate Purpose of Life, and who truly and fervently believe that they can *guarantee* their entrance into Heaven by doing certain things while on earth, will, of course, seek to do those things.

They'll make sure that their sins are confessed regularly, and that their absolutions are up-to-date, so that if they die suddenly their soul will be ready for Judgment Day. They'll fast for hours, days, or weeks at a time, travel on pilgrimages to distant holy places, go to church or temple or mosque or synagogue every week without fail, tithe 10 percent of their income, eat or not eat certain foods, wear or not wear certain clothing, say or not say certain words, and engage in all manner of rites and rituals.

They'll obey the rules of their religion, honor the customs of their faith tradition, and follow the instructions of their spiritual leaders in order to demonstrate to God that they are worthy people, so that a place will be reserved for them in Paradise.

If they are distressed enough and oppressed enough and unhappy enough, some humans will even end their own lives and kill other people—including the totally innocent and the absolutely unsuspecting—for the promise of a reward in Heaven.

(If that promised reward happens to be seventy-two black-eyed virgins with whom to spend all of eternity, and if the humans in question happen to be eighteen- to thirty-year-old men with little future and a dust-laden, poverty-stricken, injustice-filled present, the chances of their making such an extraordinarily destructive decision will increase tenfold.)

They'll do this because they believe this is *What God Wants.*

But is it?

9.

The views of humanity on so many things have been impacted by our ideas about God and about God's desires that it's hard to decide what other areas of life interaction to include in this list. The truth is, this exploration could take up an entire book. We're not going to be that expansive. We'll limit our survey to these few subjects: Male and Female, Marriage, Sex, Homosexuality, Love, Money, Free Will, Suffering, Morality, and Death.

Let's take a look at what our ancestors and our contemporary teachers have told us about these things. Let's see *What God Wants*.

Male and Female

Many humans have been told that *What God Wants* is for humanity to understand that God is male. The result is that most people who believe in a deity at all hold this to be true. The idea that God is masculine is so pervasive that it's shocking to the ear to hear God referred to as "She."

Many humans have also been told that God wants men and women to have particular roles and to be treated in particular ways in life, and that He has specified all of this in Holy Scripture.

One result of this teaching: Males are considered superior to females in nearly all of the world's cultures. In some of those cultures this manifests as cultural norms that do not allow females to go to school, to hold jobs of authority or responsibility, to leave the home without being in the company of a blood male relative, or to permit any part of their body to be seen in public, requiring them to be covered from head to toe.

(Many of these cultural restrictions are justified as honoring and protecting women, or as protecting *men* from "temptation.")

A woman's testimony in court is worth half of that of a man's—meaning that it requires two female witnesses to meet the test of adequate proof. A woman's testimony regarding a husband's beatings, cruelty, or infidelity will go ignored unless she can produce a corroborating witness, whereas a man can send his wife to death by stoning by simply stating that she committed adultery. His singular assertion is sufficient.

A woman's share of any inheritance is also accepted as being half of that of her brother. The logic behind this is that a man is financially responsible for his family, while a woman is not. This is the identical logic that, in other cultures, has blocked women from earning the same pay as men for doing the same work. The fact that a man may remain unmarried all his life and wind up not having a family, or that many women become widows, or that women would not and should not *have* to concede this role to a man if she were treated equally, is, of course, ignored by this logic.

In some male-dominant cultures, females' genitals are mutilated, cut and sewn, in order to deprive them of sexual pleasure and thus reduce the temptation they may feel to engage in sexual encounters other than those initiated by their husbands. In some cases this mutilation is seen as a rite of passage rendering female children desirable, suitable, and worthy marriage material.

Other cultural norms reflecting extreme bias against females include the custom of blocking women from becoming clergy in many religions or rising to power and authority in any civil, legal, or business enterprise, or holding any major leadership position in politics or government.

A handful of women in some cultures have overcome these customs (in many cultures they are still not allowed to even try), but always it's a struggle, always it's the notable exception, always it's a steep uphill climb to be accepted in most high-profile occupations or powerful or influential roles within the global society.

Katrina Brooks, of Rome, Georgia, knows all about that. According to an account written by Louise Chu for the Associated Press on September 25, 2004, Katrina is a member of the Southern Baptist Church who felt a calling and wanted to become a minister. She enrolled in the Baptist Theological Seminary at Richmond, Virginia, then found a church that would accept both her and her husband, Dr. Tony Brooks, who was already ordained, as co-pastors. North Rome Baptist Church in Rome, Georgia, invited the couple to lead its congregation in November 2003.

Not everyone was pleased.

A revision of the Baptist Faith and Message in 2000 takes a hard line on female pastors, Chu reports. The denomination's chief doctrinal statement says that "the office of pastor is limited to men as qualified by Scripture," citing the Bible at 1 Timothy 2:11–14. That passage reads, "Let a woman learn in silence in all submissiveness. I permit no woman to teach or to have authority over men; she is to keep silent."

Two weeks after Katrina and her husband arrived at their new church, several of her fellow clergy (all men) called meetings of the Floyd County Baptist Association to discuss the matter. They wanted the association to adopt a position that would, in effect, force the Rome church to leave the association.

This difference in the treatment of the genders is, many of the world's people believe, *What God Wants*. After all, they say the Bible says so. And so do the Scriptures of other religions.

Marriage

Many humans have been told that *What God Wants* is for marriage to be an everlasting union between a man and a woman, for better or for worse, for the purpose of propagating the species and maintaining a civil society organized into family units, which supports God's agenda for humanity.

One result of this teaching: In most religious cultures ending a marriage for whatever reason, including mental or physical cruelty, is deeply discouraged, and one major religion tells its followers that they may never divorce, may never remarry in the church nor receive the church's sacraments if they do divorce, and may never marry another person who has been divorced.

In many places and cultures marriage rules are established by religion, then become civil law, limiting and constricting the behavior of marriage partners—and those limits remain in place for life. Chief among those limits is what humans call "fidelity." Human beings living in marriage must remain faithful to each other. That is, they may not have sexual experiences with anyone else for the rest of their lives—not as a matter of personal devotion or sacred agreement, but as a matter of civil law.

This should not be surprising, since, as has just been noted, prohibitions against many kinds of private sexual activity have been placed in the common culture by religions. According to the account of these religions about *What God Wants,* human beings may not have sex with anyone outside marriage, or with anyone prior to marriage, and therefore, should they never marry, they may have sex *at no time during their entire lives.*

This is the expectation, and humans are told that the breaking of this taboo can lead to severe punishments, from God and from the social environment.

As a result, marriage is entered into by many young people around the world who are neither ready for such a commitment nor sufficiently mature for the responsibilities attached to it, but who are unwilling to endure any longer the prohibition against sexual experience.

The idea of male supremacy, drawn from the concept of God as male, has a major effect in many marriage scenarios. In some cultures marriage is considered a form of ownership and servitude, with the woman being the owned object—actually *paid for* with a dowry—and the male being the person served. Even in cultures with less extreme views, a wife is expected to be "obedient" to her husband, and to be subservient to him in every way. The man is "the head of the household."

This is, many people believe, *What God Wants.*

Sex

Many humans have been told that *What God Wants* is for sexual union to be experienced only with one's spouse for the purposes of procreation and the expression of love.

One result of this teaching: Millions of people believe that sex may absolutely never be experienced in any way that deliberately prevents conception, and that while sex is wonderful, to experience sex simply for pleasure with no possibility of procreation is against the will of God and, therefore, "unnatural," immoral, shameful, and a giving in to baser instincts.

As with the combining of fear and love in the earlier understanding of God, the combining of pleasure and shame in this construction has produced chronic emotional confusion: wonder, excitement, and passion, yet embarrassment, fear, and guilt about sexual desires and experiences.

In most cultures the sexual parts of human bodies may not be referred to by name. The words "vagina" and "penis" are not to be used in public (except as absolutely necessary in a purely clinical setting), and never with small children. The words "wee-wee," "pee-pee," or "bottom" may be used freely. In short, the human culture agrees that the actual names of certain body parts are shameful and embarrassing and are to be avoided whenever possible.

You may believe that the above assertion is a bit of an exaggeration. I assure you it is not. Internationally known columnist Molly Ivins reports in the September/October 2004 issue of *Mother Jones* magazine that Advocates for Youth, a group working for comprehensive sex education, had its funding for AIDS prevention yanked by the Centers for Disease Control, a U.S. government agency, because "young people [in the project's video] used the correct terminology for male and female anatomy." That, said James Wagoner, head of Advocates for Youth, "is absurd. What is the president going to do? Issue an executive order that every man, woman, and child should refer to the penis as a dingaling?"

And of course, if one cannot *speak* of certain body parts, one certainly cannot *show* them. Not even, apparently, to oneself. Yet another exaggeration? I'm sorry to say, no. So puritanical is the viewpoint on all of this in many places that the following letter could actually appear, without anyone blinking an eye, in over 300 newspapers in the United States on September 25, 2004, in an advice column:

> *Dear Abby,*
>
> *I went to wake up my 14-year-old daughter today and discovered her sleeping in the nude. Apparently she has been doing it for some time.*
>
> *Normally she is good about getting up and I haven't needed to enter her room to awaken her. When I asked her why she does it, she said it's more comfortable and she sleeps better.*
>
> *When I told her I was not comfortable with it, she asked me why, and frankly I could not come up with a good reason other than it seemed "wrong," and fear about what would happen in an earthquake or fire. She questioned how it could be wrong if no one knows—unless they walk into her room without knocking (as I did).*
>
> *She keeps a long robe next to the bed so she can put it on in case of emergency. (Indeed, she walks around the house in that robe, and I thought she had a nightgown underneath, when in fact she has been naked underneath since Christmas.)*

I am still not comfortable with it, but we agreed to abide by your advice. Is it OK for her to sleep in the nude, and why—or why not?

—Worried Mom in San Leandro

The columnist wrote back that there was "nothing inherently wrong" with sleeping in the nude. "Look at the bright side," she advised the mother. "It makes for less laundry."

As this parent's letter makes clear, many humans feel that certain body parts must be covered and hidden, having been deemed too arousing or too shameful, or both. For those parts not to be covered is incorrect and unacceptable. Indeed, in many places it's actually *illegal,* with punishments in *civil law* for those who fail to obey.

Many people believe that sex experienced in certain ways, even between husband and wife, is "unnatural" and therefore immoral. And again, in many times and places, some experiences, although between consenting adults, have actually been made *illegal.* Those who wrote such legislation said that they understand that God does not want certain sexual experiences to occur. God sends people to Hell for this.

Humans also believe that graphic depictions of sexual activity in photographs, drawings, comic books, video games, television, and motion pictures are distasteful, repugnant, disgusting, and unacceptable. Graphic depictions of extreme physical violence and killing are, however, entirely acceptable.

Millions of humans believe that sexual energy and spiritual energy do not mix. They have been told that sexual energy is a "lower chakra" energy, and that sexual activity and spiritual clarity essentially oppose each other. Persons seeking to achieve spiritual mastery are therefore advised against engaging in sexual experiences. Some are actually required to remain abstinent.

This is, many of the world's people believe, *What God Wants.*

Homosexuality

Many humans have been told that *What God Wants* is for sex to be experienced between a male and a female only, and for same-gender sexual interaction to be considered an abomination.

One result of this teaching: Humans for whom same-gender sexual attraction feels most natural have been denounced, vilified, condemned, ostracized, isolated, assaulted, and killed by people who believe they are doing God's will.

The sad account of the killing of Matthew Shepard in Laramie, Wyoming, offers us a now-famous case in point. Shepard, an openly gay freshman at the University of Wyoming, was dragged out of a bar in Laramie by two young men, driven to a deserted road outside of town, tied to a cow fence, and beaten so severely that he lapsed into a coma and died five days later.

His youthful assailants were apprehended and sentenced to life in prison, but the Reverend Fred Phelps, pastor of the Westboro Baptist Church of Topeka, Kansas, was not inclined to let the matter rest there. Every year for the five years following Matthew's brutal beating and death, this Christian minister has traveled to Laramie, as well as to Casper, Wyoming, Matthew's birthplace, to "celebrate" his death. And, according to a report in the *Los Angeles Times* by reporter David Kelly, on October 12, 2003, Reverend Phelps brought with him to Casper a granite monument engraved with Matthew's face, followed by these words chiseled in stone:

MATTHEW SHEPARD ENTERED HELL OCTOBER 12, 1998, AT AGE 21 IN DEFIANCE OF GOD'S WARNING: "THOU SHALT NOT LIE WITH MANKIND AS WITH WOMANKIND; IT IS ABOMINATION."

—LEVITICUS 18:32

It was the Reverend Phelps who also attended Matthew Shepard's funeral and, as the young man's parents, family, and friends stood in mourning, screamed: "God hates fags!"

With this level of clarity as to Divine Intention and Desire, entire countries have been forced under power of governmental authority and rule of law to obey God's Will in this matter. In some nations the civil penalty for homosexuality is death—burial under a twelve-foot concrete wall. In many places civil law has been created making gay marriage illegal. In the United States the president in 2004 personally campaigned to have his understanding of God's desires regarding prohibition of gay marriage written into his country's constitution. (As one nationally syndicated newspaper columnist wrote, the irony here is that committed gay couples are desperately trying to *do* what straight couples are desperately trying to *avoid*.)

While certain sexual feelings may be very natural to the persons feeling them, they are not *What God Wants,* many people say, and are therefore by *definition* "unnatural." A report on October 20, 2003, by Chris Zdeb of CanWest News Service in the *Calgary Herald* in Edmonton, Canada, points to the possibility that the exact opposite may be true.

"Scientists have discovered 54 genes that suggest sexual identity is hard-wired into the brain before birth, and before development of the sex organs," the journalist reports, and goes on to say, "The findings released today by a team of University of California, Los Angeles, researchers could mean that sexuality, including homosexuality and transgender sexuality, are not a choice."

Nevertheless, the clergy of many of the world's largest religious denominations continue to assert that God condemns such sexual experiences.

Jerry Falwell Ministries issued a statement on October 6, 1999, which it described as its "definitive stance on homosexuality."

The statement said that "to suggest that homosexuality is a physical condition caused by biological facts rather than an emotional and mental condition is highly blasphemous. The Bible tells us that the cause of homosexuality is sin. A person is not born a homosexual; he becomes one according to his sinful will. A person lets sin and the devil take control of his life."

Gays, say the folks at Jerry Falwell Ministries, "are unsaved people." They are "sure to go to Hell unless they repent of that sin and forsake it, and turn to the Lord Jesus Christ for forgiveness."

And reporter Rachel Zoll of the Associated Press reported on October 7, 2004, that the most influential Anglican leader in Africa—home to nearly half the world's Anglicans—said that the U.S. Episcopal Church has created a "new religion" by confirming a gay bishop in New Hampshire, breaking the bonds between the denominations with roots in the Church of England.

Archbishop Peter Akinola of Nigeria also said in an exclusive AP interview with Zoll that he views the head of the Episcopal Church as an advocate for gays and lesbians and no longer trusts him. His comments came less than two weeks before an international panel was scheduled to release a critical report on whether the global Anglican Communion can bridge its divide over homosexuality. The Episcopal Church is the U.S. branch of Anglicanism; Akinola leads the Anglican Church of Nigeria.

"The Communion is shattered. It is broken," Akinola said. "The commonality that bound us together is no longer true." (More separation in the name of God.)

Zoll's report says that Akinola insisted he did not hate gays, despite his fiery comments in the past protesting the growing acceptance of homosexuality. He once called the trend a "satanic attack" on the church. But he said he could not accept attempts to "superimpose" modern culture on Scripture by ignoring what he said were biblical injunctions against gay sex.

"I didn't write the Bible. It's part of our Christian heritage. It tells us what to do," Akinola said. "If the word of God says homosexuality is an abomination, then so be it."

The Zoll story goes on to say that those who support ordaining gays contend Scripture does not ban same-sex relationships, and that there was no understanding in biblical times that homosexuality was, as science is now proving, a natural orientation, not a choice.

Nevertheless, for many of the world's people the Afterlife consequence of engaging in what they declare to be "unnatural activities" is understood to be everlasting damnation and torture in the fires of Hell.

This is, those people believe, *What God Wants.*

Love

Many humans have been told that *What God Wants* is for love to be conditional. God has made it clear that He loves humans if they do what He wants. If they do not, humans shall know His wrath. They'll be condemned to everlasting damnation.

Some say that God is acting with love when He condemns people to eternal and unending torture. With this explanation they seek to preserve the image and the notion of a loving God.

One result of this teaching: Many people are very

confused about the true nature of love. Human beings "get," at some deeply intuitive level, that the imposing of unending punishment is not a loving thing to do. Yet they are told that such punishment is a demonstration of the purest and highest love. It's God's love in action.

It's not unusual for human beings to therefore be afraid of love, even as they have been made afraid of God, who is the source of love. They have been taught that God's love can turn into wrath in a flicker, producing horrifying results. This packaging of love and fear in human theology has not been without consequences in human behavior.

Earlier it was said, "Humanity's ideas about God produce humanity's ideas about life and about people." This is profoundly true, and thus, many humans are afraid of and attracted to love at the same time. Often their first thought upon moving into a closer love relationship with another is, "Now what is this person going to want, or need, or expect from me?" That is, after all, the nature of their love relationship with an all-powerful God, and they have no reason to believe it will be any different with a much weaker human being.

There is also the corollary thought that partners in a relationship have a *right* to expect certain things in exchange for love—that love is a give-and-take, quid pro quo proposition.

These expectations and fears undermine many love relationships at the outset.

Because love and the worst torture imaginable have been linked in the minds of humans as natural activities on the part of God, most humans believe that it's right and proper to punish other humans for their behaviors—just as God does.

In perhaps the most dramatic demonstration of this, many human beings believe that it's appropriate to kill human beings to send a message to human beings that it's inappropriate to kill human beings.

This is, many of the world's people believe, *What God Wants.*

Money

Many humans have been told that *What God Wants* is for money to be considered the root of all evil. Money is bad, and God is good, and so money and God do not mix.

One result of this teaching: The higher one's purpose and the greater one's value to society, the lower one's income must be. Nurses, teachers, public safety officials, and those in similar service professions are not to ask to make much money. Ministers, rabbis, and priests are to ask even less. Homemakers and mothers, under this guideline, should have no personal income at all. If they want something for themselves, they may ask their husband for a few dollars, or scrimp pennies from the grocery money.

The message here is: Because "filthy lucre" is bad, because money is intrinsically evil, pay must be in reverse proportion to the value of the function performed. The better the deed, the worse the pay. People should not get lots of money for doing good things. And if they're doing something really, really, *really* good, they should want to do it for free.

Humans have created a disconnect between "doing good" and being well compensated. On the other hand, doing things of somewhat less lasting intrinsic value can produce compensation in the millions. So can illegal activity of all kinds. Thus, society's values discourage noble actions and encourage triviality and illegality. Humanity's watchword is: The higher the purpose, the lower the reward.

This is, many of the world's people believe, *What God Wants.*

10.

How are you doing here? I know this is taking a while, but it's important for us to periodically look at these things. The influence of the teachings we have all received about God runs deep. It embraces philosophical areas as well as the practical aspects of life.

Even though the final topics we touch upon here revolve around concepts that we may think we'll encounter only in the abstract, the fact is that how we think about these abstractions affects—and *creates*—our very concrete moment-to-moment experience.

Free Will

Many humans have been told that *What God Wants* is for human beings to have Free Will. Thus, they may determine and decide for themselves which of the Ultimate Outcomes—Heaven or Hell—they will experience after their death. They may do as they choose at any moment, at every juncture. They are not restricted in any way.

Humans have been told that God has granted humanity this Free Will so that humans may freely choose God, freely choose God's Way, and freely choose to be reunited with God in Heaven. In other words, they may freely choose to be good, as opposed to being forced to do so. God wants humans to return to God by *choice*. No one should be required to do so.

Human beings have also been told that under the doctrine of Free Will, while people may do as they choose, if they do not choose *What God Wants* they'll pay for it with continuous torture through all eternity. No element of duress is seen in this. It's simply the Way Things Are. It's Justice, at the highest level. It's God's Justice, which follows God's Judgment. It's important, therefore, to freely choose *What God Wants*.

One result of this teaching: Humanity's concept of freedom has been deeply affected and profoundly shaped by its understanding of what God means by "freedom." Humans have decided that freedom doesn't have to mean *freedom*, but can mean simply the ability to select outcomes. This is better than having no choice at all, and so humans in positions of power have learned to use the word "freedom" to privately describe the process by which they get others to do as they are told. People don't have to do as they are told, of course. But if they do not, there will be a price to pay. That could mean anything from having taxes audited to being thrown in jail for two years without charges being filed and without any explanation other than being labeled a threat to the security of the country. Using this measure, nations call themselves "free."

Most people, except, perhaps, the most stubborn apologists, see the contradiction in all of this. They understand perfectly well that no people are truly free who face the most horrendous outcomes imaginable if they don't do what they're told. Only a hypocrite or a fool would call such a choice "free."

Humans have learned, then, that hypocrisy—especially hypocrisy for the "right" purpose, in the "right" cause—is acceptable on earth as it is in Heaven. Much of humanity's political activity has been informed by this ethic. And elsewhere within the spectrum of human activity as well, in the way many humans communicate with each other, in the way many deal with each other, it has come to be understood that the end justifies the means.

In fact, many humans have now convinced themselves that none of this is hypocrisy at all. It's simply a matter of *interpretation.*

And so, in this day and age, freedoms are taken away in the name of Freedom itself. Millions of people gratefully embrace the political rhetoric that says *lack* of freedom is what guarantees their freedom, and the religious doctrine that says their choices in life are free only if they do as they are told, because this is *What God Wants.*

Suffering

Many humans have been told that *What God Wants* is for suffering to be used by human beings to better themselves, and to purify their soul. Suffering is good. It earns credits, or points, in God's mind, especially if it's endured silently, and maybe even "offered up" to God. Suffering is a necessary part of human growth and learning and is, more importantly, a means by which people may be redeemed in the eyes of God.

Indeed, one whole religion is built on this belief, asserting that all beings have been saved by the suffering of one being, who died for the sins of the rest. This one being paid the "debt" said to be owed to God for humanity's weakness and wickedness. According to this doctrine, God has been hurt by the weakness and wickedness of humanity, and in order to set things straight, *someone has to suffer.* Otherwise, God and humanity could not be reconciled. Thus, suffering has been established as a redemptive experience.

With regard to the suffering of human beings due to "natural" causes, it's not to be shortened by death under any circumstances that are not also "natural." The suffering of animals may be mercifully ended before "natural" death, but not the suffering of people. It's God and God alone who determines when human suffering shall end.

One result of this teaching: Human beings have endured unimaginable suffering over extended periods in order to do God's will and not incur God's wrath in the Afterlife. Millions of people feel that even if a person is very, very old and is suffering very, very much—lingering on the verge of death but not dying, experiencing interminable pain instead—that person must endure whatever life is bringing them.

Humanity has actually created civil law declaring that people have no right to end their own suffering, nor may they assist another in ending theirs. However anguishing it may be, however otherwise hopeless a life may have become, the suffering must go on.

This is *What God Wants.*

Morality

Many humans have been told that *What God Wants* is a moral society.

One result of this teaching: Humanity has spent its entire history attempting to define what is moral and what is not. The challenge has been to come up with a standard for society that does not change, all the while the society itself is changing. To find this "gold standard," many societies have turned to God, or Allah, or Yahweh, or Jehovah, or whatever other name they have used to designate Deity, and have relied on their understanding of *What God Wants*.

Many centuries ago God's preferences in this matter were given a powerful label. They were called "natural." This is because the concept of a Deity first entered the minds of primitive humans as a result of their earliest observations of and contacts with Nature. Here was something bigger than they were, something they could not control, something they could only stand by and watch, hoping for the best.

"Hoping for the best" soon transmuted into what would now be called praying. Whoever and whatever this Deity was, early humans reasoned, it was deeply connected with Nature, and Nature was an expression of It. And so humans created gods representing the sun, moon, and stars, the weather, crops, rivers, the land, and nearly everything else, in hopes of getting some control over things—or at least getting some communication going with whoever *did* have control.

From this connection of God and Nature it was only a short mental hop to consider that all things having to do with deities and gods were "natural," and all things not having anything to do with deities were "unnatural." When human language came into form the words "God" and "Nature" became inextricably linked. Certain conditions, circumstances, and behaviors were then described as "natural" or "unnatural," depending upon whether they adhered to or violated the current perception of the Will of God.

That which is "unnatural" has, in turn, come to be described as "immoral"—since it's not of God, and cannot, therefore, be *What God Wants*. The circle thus completes itself. Anything that is not considered "natural" is considered "immoral." That includes all "unnatural" abilities, powers, behaviors—and even thoughts.

The idea that *What God Wants* is what is natural, and that what is natural is what is moral, has not been a perfect measure, but it has been the best that humanity has been able to do in the search for an unchanging standard. It's for this reason that humanity has been loath to change its ideas about *What God Wants*. Changing those ideas changes the gold standard of human behavior.

Behavior is the currency of human interaction. Beliefs about *What God Wants* give value to the behavioral choices of humans, just as gold gives value to the pieces of paper called money.

Thus, in most human societies it's not an individual's actual experience, but the society's *definition* of it, that determines its morality. This is the case with homosexuality. It's also the case with a great many other behaviors, such as prostitution, premarital sex, depictions of explicit sexual activity, the use of peyote, marijuana, and other plants and stimulants, or even the experience of ecstasy not induced by any outside stimulant.

For instance, if one says one has had an ecstatic experience of God, but if the experience does not fall within what humanity currently defines as "natural," it's considered immoral and to be warned against and, if it's continued, to be condemned, and, if it's still continued, to be punished.

In previous times such an experience was often punishable by torture or death. More than one saint claiming and describing such ecstasies has been martyred in humanity's long history, using such guidelines.

Those saints were killed because the people killing them were convinced that they were doing *What God Wants.*

Death

Many humans have been told that *What God Wants* is for their wonderful life to eventually end, at which time their opportunity to learn and to grow is over and the time to be rewarded or punished for how they have lived begins.

One result of this teaching: Many humans consider that death is a terrible thing, and something to be feared. It's the End of the Line, the Final Curtain Call, the Closing Bell. Nearly all of the imageries surrounding death are negative, fearful, or sad, not positive, uplifting, or joyful. These imageries pervade our society. A street that goes nowhere is a Dead End. A person who is badly mistaken is Dead Wrong. The spirit who comes to retrieve your soul is the Grim Reaper.

Most people do not want to even talk about death, much less experience it. No one wants to experience it before he or she has to. People cling to life, sometimes desperately. The survival instinct is the strongest human instinct of all. Our common culture supports survival as the ultimate goal. Even people who *want* to die are not allowed to.

On the other side of death, many people feel certain, is the Final Judgment. If you have not been good, it's at this point that you'll go to Hell. Your payment for all of your sins in this way is *What God Wants.*

Humanity's list of *What God Wants* is very long and covers many other areas of human experience not discussed here. That list forms the basis of innumerable civil laws, cultural traditions, social mores, and familial customs that touch all human beings.

So what do you think about what you've read here? With allowances for a few exceptions in wording here and there, or a slight difference in interpretation, is this basically what you remember being taught about *What God Wants?*

If it is, you have a lot of company. Millions of people have had the same experience.

Nay, billions.

What if something very important that humans think they know about God is simply inaccurate?

Would that change anything?

11.

Now let me ask you if you noticed something that I've noticed about what we've all been taught about *What God Wants*. Did you notice that the theology represented by our traditional teachings is a theology of separation? In this theology, we are over here, and God is over there.

Well, yes, you might say, but that's how it is, isn't it?

If we think theology does not really affect our everyday lives that much, the answer to this question almost wouldn't matter. You would believe what you believe, and I would believe what I believe, and others would believe what they believe, and we'd all go our ways with our beliefs and live our lives. But this is not simply a theological issue.

Theology produces sociology.

A theology of separation produces a sociology of separation.

It is as simple as that. Regrettably, theology too often produces a sociology that produces pathology.

That is exactly what has happened all over the earth. Humanity has created, and we now live in, a pathology of separation. Separation from God and separation from each other.

Now it's true that in spite of our sociology of separation, we have made some remarkable achievements. Human beings can split the atom, create a cure for disease, send a man to the moon, and crack the genetic code of life itself. Yet, sadly, many people—perhaps the largest number—cannot do the simplest thing.

Get along.

Why is this, do you imagine?

Think about this.

With all that humans have been taught through their myths, in their cultural stories, and by their religions—with all that humans have been told about God and about Life by their ancestors and their elders and their ministers and their priests and their rabbis and their mullahs—how is it that, in the collective experience of a huge portion of humanity, *it hasn't done any more good?*

But it has done a lot of good, you may say. The world *is* a better place than it was before. People do not act as they did in primitive times. They live in peace in most places, and they are not violent.

No, they are not. Most individuals are not. We can agree on that. But can we agree on this? *Collectively,* humanity is unceasingly and increasingly violent with its own kind.

Allowing people to go hungry is a form of violence.

Placing life-saving drugs and the finest medical care out of reach of millions is a form of violence.

Underpaying laborers while taking huge front-office profits is a form of violence.

Mistreating, underpaying, denying promotions to, and mutilating females is a form of violence.

Racial prejudice is a form of violence.

Child abuse, child labor, child slavery, child prostitution, child trafficking, and child soldiering is a form of violence.

The death penalty is a form of violence.

Denying civil rights to people because of their sexual preference or their religion or their ethnicity is a form of violence.

Creating and maintaining a worldwide society in which exploitation, oppression, and injustice are commonplace is a form of violence.

Ignoring suffering is as much a form of violence as inducing it.

In 2004 humanity watched more than 75,000 people die and over 1.5 million forced from their homes during ethnic fighting in the Darfur region of Sudan. The world stalled and stumbled and did little or nothing for many months as this went on. That is the mark of an extraordinarily primitive society, too timid, too weak, too stultified, or worse yet, too self-involved to be able to put a quick stop *even to genocide.*

Are you growing a little impatient with the narrative here? I don't blame you. It's tough to look at how things are, at how they *really* are, in our world. We'd like to stay on the sunny side of things. We'd like to keep thinking positively, keep feeling good about life. No one wants to look at the bad stuff.

But if we don't spend at least a *little* bit of time looking at the bad stuff, how are we going to change it? Is the best way to change something to not acknowledge that it's there?

I don't think so. There's a line in the wonderful Arthur Miller play *Death of a Salesman* in which Linda, the outraged wife of Willy Loman, cries out to her grown sons to *notice* the tragedy before them in the form of a father whose life is crumbling right in front of their eyes, and to notice what he has gone through in life, and what he has tried to give them. "Attention must be paid," she says with shaking voice. *"Attention must be paid."*

We need to pay attention to the fact that our way of life is dying. We need to notice what the world has gone through, and what it has tried to give us. And we need to notice what we are doing, collectively and individually, in that world.

Attention must be paid.

In our world today an estimated 250 million children are working. Of these, more than 50 million between the ages of five and eleven are engaged in intolerable forms of labor, according to the United Nations Children's Fund's 2000 report, *The Progress of Nations*. Does anybody care?

At any one time more than 300,000 children under eighteen, girls and boys, are fighting as soldiers with government armed forces and armed opposition groups in more than thirty countries worldwide, according to the *Global Report on Child Soldiers* (2001), published by the Coalition to Stop the Use of Child Soldiers. While most child soldiers are aged between fifteen and eighteen, the youngest age recorded in this report is seven.

For nearly two-thirds of the world's people, life is a daily struggle. For half of that number, it's a struggle for *survival*. Does anybody care?

Why do these conditions exist, do you think? Do you think it might have anything to do with the fact that we don't see each other on this earth as members of the same family? Do you think it may be because we imagine that we are separate from each other?

For whatever the reason, the fact is that the world has not put into place a system for sharing the abundance of the earth that works for everyone, only for those who meet certain criteria of skin color or gender or religion or ethnicity.

The UN reports that donor countries allocate an average of just one-quarter of one percent (0.25 percent) of their total gross national product to development assistance for poorer nations. Does anybody care?

And what is the stingiest developed nation in the world in terms of the proportion of total wealth that it donates? The United States, arguably the world's richest country. The richest is the stingiest.

Can this be possible? Yes. It's possible, and it's true.

Now you might say, Hey, wait a minute, the United States puts in more dollars than half of the other countries combined. And you'd be right. In actual dollars, you're right. But the United States *has* more dollars than half the other countries combined. So, as a *portion of what it has,* the United States is the stingiest of all.

If you have ten dollars, and you give your brother three because he is in trouble, and if your neighbor has fifty dollars, and he gives his brother five, which one of you is more generous? Are you impressed by the fact that your neighbor gave more in actual numbers than you? Or are you mindful of the fact that he has five times as much as you, and therefore he could have given five times more? It might have been hoped that he would give in proportion to his wealth, don't you think?

My own idea about this is echoed in the words of John F. Kennedy many years ago: "Of those to whom much is given, much is asked."

But the United States is not alone in underprioritizing allocations for nations in need. All of the world's richest countries in 2003 spent $60 billion to help the poorest countries address the problems of poverty, lack of education, and poor health. During the same period the spending of these richest countries for defense was *$900 billion.*

This led the president of the World Bank to suggest dryly that if the world simply reversed its priorities, the cost of defense would never have to exceed the smaller sum.

In a global society where the suffering of others really mattered—not just at the level of lip service, but at the level of *doing something about it* that actually changes things—such a reversal of priorities would be instant and automatic.

Because that shift in priorities has not taken place, violence of a more direct kind is becoming a way of life on the earth. More and more often these days, in more and more places, it takes the form of direct physical attacks by one person or group upon another.

The sign of a social order that is failing is that even among those people in the world whose lives are more comfortable and who are not overtly suffering, violence is on a dramatic upswing. When even those who should be contented are discontented, you know something's wrong; you know you're in trouble.

Violence is on the upswing not only on the streets of the Middle East, but on the streets of Europe; not only in the homes of the poor in Southeast Asia, but in the homes of the well-to-do in North America. That is why now in many countries metal detectors are found everywhere—at military installations and airports, where they might be expected, but also at places where they would once have been considered grotesquely out of place: shopping malls and hotels, department stores and nightclubs, and yes, even schools, churches, mosques, temples, and synagogues.

That is why in London there are hidden cameras on the streets. It is said that the average person is photographed 300 times a day in London. In Chicago it has just been announced that hundreds of new street cameras are being installed throughout the city, adding to the thousands already there. All of this is for our protection, of course. It is about security. These cameras are programmed by computer to pick up any "unusual activity" and to send an alarm to police, fire, and other agencies, which will dispatch personnel at once.

Big Brother is watching you.

George Orwell gave that chilling description of everyday life on our planet in a book he wrote over fifty years ago. It took his nightmare world of 1984 twenty years longer than expected to be created, but created it has been, complete with global positioning satellites that can pinpoint a person's location within fifty feet, on-street surveillance cameras, government access to video rental and library withdrawal records, and, in fact, scrutiny of virtually any kind of activity you undertake outside your home. Soon there may be cameras *in* your home. Does anybody care?

All of this is necessary, we are told, because increasing numbers of people everywhere have become frustrated, angry, disaffected, unpredictable, and more willing than ever to use violence.

Why is this, do you imagine?

Think about this.

And why have human theologies, to which humanity looks for the wisest answers to life's most difficult questions, been unable to reverse this trend—to say nothing of heading it off in the first place?

The answer is that Separation Theology does not work. Yet people insist, to this moment, that it is *What God Wants.*

12.

If you are really interested in *What God Wants,* let me ask you a question. In your opinion, have our earthly theologies provided humanity with effective guidance in how to live together in peace and harmony?

Here's my opinion: No. In fact, far too often they have produced just the opposite result.

Today 400 children die of starvation every hour. *Every hour.* Yet it would be possible to feed all the starving children on the planet, to protect them from dying of preventable diseases, and to make basic education accessible to all with no more than 5 percent of the overall annual sales of arms in the world.

Five percent.

Can this be possible?

Yes. It's possible, and it's true.

How is this evidence of a failure of religions and theologies? Neglect of its own offspring to the point of starvation could only occur in a society whose people see themselves as separate from God and separate from each other, having little to do with each other, *and this is what is taught by our religions.* Only such a cultural story could justify a world in which the income of the richest 225 people is equal to the income of three billion poor people.

You may have missed the real impact of that, so let me say it again. We have created a world in which the income of the richest 225 people is equal to the income of three billion poor people.

Three billion.

That's half the world's population.

What's so wrenchingly sad about all of this is not only that the situation exists, but that so many people think it's *okay* that it exists. You tell them that the income of the richest 225 people is equal to the income of three billion poor people, and they say, "Uh-huh. Okay. So what's the problem?"

Want to know why there's so much unrest and violence in the world today? Open your eyes.

Perhaps you already have. Perhaps you already know. Perhaps you understand. Yet it will take more people understanding, and then deciding to do something about what they understand, for anything to change. If only more of us could open our eyes to the world around us! If only more of us could create our world as an expression of our oneness. If only our theologies could help more of us do more of this more of the time. But in fact it is our theologies that keep us from experiencing the reality of our oneness, and teach us of separation. And it is our ideas of separation that allow such conditions to continue to exist.

If theology was a physical science—biology, say, or physics—its data would long ago have been judged unreliable in producing consistent results, even after thousands of years. At the very least, that data would now be questioned.

Does humanity have the courage to question its own data about life and about God? Are humans brave enough to ponder the unaskable *What if*?

What if something very important that humans think they know about God is simply inaccurate? Would that change anything?

How much more will people allow themselves to endure before they begin looking for the underlying reason that the world is the way it is? And, of those people who say that a belief in God is powerful enough to be the cure for the world's ills, how many are able to see that an *inaccurate* belief could be powerful enough to be the *cause*?

How about you? Where are you with all of this? Given the state of the world today, do you think this may be a good moment to consider some new thoughts about God, about life, and about each other?

How is your own life going? Are things just fine? Or are you meeting more challenges than, frankly, you'd like to be encountering in your relationships, in your career, in your day-to-day movement through life?

As you look at your life and as you look at the world around you, do you think you are seeing a reflection of *What God Wants?* If not, what do you think that God *does* want?

Yes, well, I suppose that's why you picked up this book, isn't it . . . ?

I mean, you picked up this book to see what it had to say on this subject, yes? So now it's time to say it. Now it's time to reveal the great truth about *What God Wants.* This could well be the most important information ever placed before the human race. It has been placed there in the past, more than once, but the human race has not seemed to understand it. It is now going to be revealed so clearly, so plainly, in such a new and accessible way, that there can be no possibility of future misunderstanding.

Because this information is so vital to humanity's future, the entire next chapter has been devoted to it.

But before you turn the page, a note of caution, please. The revelation here may shock you. Humanity has held its ideas and beliefs about *What God Wants* close to its collective heart for thousands of generations.

I said, *thousands of generations.*

That's a very long time. For a species that claims to love adventure, humans are remarkably resistant to the new. And when it comes to that which is oldest in the universe—presumed by some to *predate* the universe, and to have *created* it—this is doubly true.

So don't be surprised if you are resistant to the breathtaking revelation on the next page. Yet now is the time for change—and the next chapter could be much more than a new chapter in this book. It could be a new chapter in your life.

So let us now courageously explore together the truth about *What God Wants. . . .*

13.

14.

You've just seen the answer to the most important question in human history.

What does God want?

Nothing.

Absolutely nothing at all.

Please think about this.

No, really. Don't just plow ahead, impatient to see where this book is going from here, or toss it away, convinced that it has nothing after all to say to you. Please. Just stop for a moment. Will you? Will you just stop?

Thank you. Now I'm going to ask you to quietly ponder what has just been said here. Place the book gently in your lap, close your eyes for a second, and contemplate this idea:

What does God want?

Nothing.
Absolutely nothing at all.

How does that feel to you? How does that thought feel when you try it on?

Does it produce an empty feeling? Does it produce anger? Does it produce simple agreement, as in "ho-hum, nothing new"? Does it confuse you? Does it make you happy?

How do you think the world at large would react if it turned out to be true? What, if anything, do you think would change?

(The answer to that last question might surprise you. We're going to take a look at that here.)

Can there be any kind of meaningful theology if we have a God who wants nothing?

If we say that God wants nothing, are we as much as saying that there is no God at all? If we all agree that there *is* a God, but that there is nothing God wants, then what is God up to? What is God's purpose and function? Why believe in God? Who needs one?

Some people have come to these questions and

walked away shrugging their shoulders, saying, "There *is* no reason to believe in God. We *don't* need one."

I would argue strenuously that the first of those above two statements is false, and the second is true. There is a reason—and a very good one—to believe in God, and . . . we don't need God.

The reason to believe in God is that this belief opens us to the possibility of God's power playing a role in our lives. You can't use the power of God if you can't believe in the existence of that power.

Yet why would we care about using the power of God if we don't need God? Fair question. The very fact that we *can* use the power of God is why we don't need God. The answer is circular. If a rich man writes you into his will, in which he says he has given you all of his money, placing it in a safe deposit box for you, then you don't need that man. Yet if you don't believe the man ever existed, you will not even go to the safe deposit box to get the money. *You won't believe the money is there.* You'll think it's all a ruse, a farce. You'll be rich and won't know it.

God made us "in the image and likeness of God." This is a *truth*. This is not just a nice statement, it is what is *so*. It is as the Scriptures tell us: "Have I not said, Ye are gods?"

The idea that we need God is an illusion. It is an act

of forgetfulness. It is what we imagine is true when we forget who we really are, rejecting our inheritance. If our belief in God is based on the idea that we need God for some reason, then most of our interactions with God will be dysfunctional. And, of course, they are. That's the point here.

The very *best* reason to believe in God is that we don't need God. God has made us capable enough to get along just fine, as any good parent would. Thus, we can be open to just loving God—and just loving God is the most powerful thing any of us could ever do. That's because love unleashes the power of who we are, and when that power is unleashed, there is nothing we cannot do. Which is, of course, what God intended.

God did not intend for us to be dependent on Him. God intended for us to be *independent*. Free. And not only free, but *fully capable*. Of what? Of producing, of creating, of experiencing, what we have long desired.

But just loving God means, of course, that we would stop fearing God—and that could happen only if we thought we did not need God. So long as we imagine that we need God for something, we invite fear, because we believe that there is always a chance that God will not give us what we need.

Most of humanity's interactions with God are dysfunctional precisely because most of humanity has created a need-based relationship with God. This relationship not only assumes that we need something from God but, perhaps of more profound implication, that *God needs something from us.*

The relationship with God that so many people on earth have established falls apart if it is true that God wants nothing at all from human beings. Yet that the relationship falls apart does not mean the relationship has ended. Sometimes things need to fall apart for things to truly fall together for the first time. It does not always serve us to shy away from ideas that may cause things to fall apart. So let's look again, and now more deeply, at this idea:

What does God want?

Nothing.

Absolutely nothing at all.

Please think about this. Even if you disagree with this vehemently, think about it. *Especially* if you disagree, please think about it deeply.

What makes you disagree?

Who told you that this statement could not be true?

What makes *them* right?

How do you know that *they* know what is true? Because they read it in a book? Fair enough. But then, *what makes the book right?* Because God said it was right? *Which* God? Which *book?*

Think about this deeply, if only for the intellectual, emotional, and spiritual exercise.

Let's pretend just for the moment that it's true that God wants nothing from humanity. If that is so, then virtually all of life's applecarts are upended. Ancient myths are upended. Cultural stories are upended. Ethnic customs are upended. Familial traditions are upended. Religious doctrines are upended. Legal systems and educational systems are upended. Political, economic, and social constructions of every kind are upended.

Could this be the reason that the idea of a God who wants something has been perpetuated?

Think about this.

Why would God want anything? What is it that God could possibly want or need? What would *cause* God to want or need anything? What could cause God to become unhappy if He did not get it?

Now think about *this* . . .

What could cause God *to make humans responsible* for His getting what He wants? Would you make your children responsible for your happiness?

We have been told of a God who wants humans to love Him, to worship Him, to adore Him, to surrender to Him, to be grateful to Him, and to pay Him homage. *Why?* Why would God want this? Why would God care?

We have been told of a God who wants humans to

keep His commandments, and if they do not, and if they fail to seek and obtain forgiveness in the proper and pre-scribed manner, He then wants them to go to Hell, there to suffer intolerable anguish. But think about this. Why would God punish humans so horribly for their confu-sion and weakness?

If *we* wanted someone to understand *us* better and to obey *us* always and in everything, and if we just could not get them to do it, would we make it their fault?

(Well, of course, we would and we do. But who can blame us? We are using God as our model. Yet what if our model is based on faulty assumptions?)

We have been told of a God whose justice is perfect. Yet why would a God who is vulnerable to nothing and cannot be hurt or damaged in any way need to punish anyone for anything, much less *sentence them to torture?*

We have been told of a God who wants and invites humans to go to battle for Him, to kill others for Him, just as He has been recorded in the Scriptures as having killed thousands who incurred His wrath. But why? Why would God kill anybody, or ask others to kill in His name?

Does God really want humans to massacre others while fighting for His Cause? What *is* His Cause, anyway?

What is God up to? What is "God's Cause"?

Is it to get everybody on earth to join a single reli-gion? Is that it? *Is that What God Wants?*

Why? Why would God want that? Why would God care?

Does it really matter to God whether you are a Muslim or a Jew, a Hindu or a Christian, a Buddhist or a Bahá'í? What if you are a good person, a kind, caring, compassionate, and loving individual, but are a member of no organized religion at all?

What if you actually speak out *against* organized religions and their extremes? Does that make you an apostate? Does that mean you are doomed? Does that make you an infidel and render you eligible to be killed by a True Believer? *Is this What God Wants?*

Why? Why does it matter? Who *told* you that it mattered? *Was it the organized religion that wants you to be its member?*

Think about this.

Is this the purpose of religion on the earth? Is this the Cause of God?

What happens to all of this, what becomes of this entire thought system, if it's declared that God wants nothing, *nothing at all,* from human beings?

Can you believe in a God who wants nothing? Is it possible to hold such a thought in your reality?

Can you even *imagine it?*

15.

Consider the possibility that most of the world's people hold an inaccurate belief about God. Consider the possibility that the truth about God is something that most people can't even imagine.

For instance, wouldn't it be interesting if there was no such thing as the Will of God? Wouldn't that change a lot of things?

Do you think that it's God's Will that the world is the way it is? And if it's *not* God's Will, is God powerless to do anything about it? And if God is *not* powerless to do anything about it, why isn't God doing something about it? And if God *is* doing something about it, why isn't God succeeding?

Some say it's because *humanity isn't letting Him.* Humanity is standing in the way of God getting *What God Wants.* Actually, more than a few people believe this. According to this doctrine, God is unable to achieve *What God Wants,* and humanity is at fault. Yet unless there is something that humans don't understand about who and what God is, isn't there a breakdown in logic somewhere?

Perhaps here is where Satan comes in. It's as good a place as any, and it's a convenient place for sure. Perhaps this whole business is all part of God's battle with Satan for men's souls. Perhaps it's God Himself who allows things to happen that are against God's Will, in order for the struggle with Satan to be played out. Yet if that is true, then it's *God's Will* that God's Will be violated . . . in which case God's Will is not being violated at all.

Could it be that God's Will is *always being expressed,* simply in differing form?

So what, then, IS God's Will? And how can we know it?

Here we go again. How can human beings know *What God Wants?*

Perhaps it's time for a more pointed question. Do you think it's possible that we're simply making this all up? At the very least, do you think it's possible that there's something we don't understand about God, *the understanding of which could change everything?*

I believe the answer to both questions is yes. And here is what most humans and most religions are afraid to look at: Perhaps what it is that humans don't understand about God is that God is not at all what people have thought.

Perhaps God is not an old man in the sky with needs and desires, a personal will and personal fears, and all the inner conflicts, contradictions, turmoil, and emotional turbulence of humans. Perhaps God is the Sum Total of Everything—truly the "All in All," the "Alpha and the Omega," "That Which IS"—and perhaps *nothing stands outside of this.*

If that is true, then YOU do not stand outside of This, and This does not stand outside of you. This means that what you want, God wants. It means that your will for you is God's will for you.

Yet what happens when we are of the consciousness "not as I will, but Thy will be done"? What happens when we make a choice to have God choose for us, and God is saying, "You may do as you wish"? What happens to the will, to the idea, to the request then, if we say to God, You choose for us, but God is saying, *You* choose for *you?*

When you make a choice to have God choose for you, you have essentially taken down the sail, let go of the rudder, and set your boat adrift on a stormy sea. This is because God really and truly does choose for you what you choose for you. Or, to put this all another way, if God did have a preference, this, in fact, would be it: that you get to choose.

Now if you do not *want* to choose, if you want someone else to do the choosing *for* you, we have a small problem here. You can, of course, give up your future to fate, but the winds of fate, as you must surely have learned, can take you in either of two directions: into safe harbor, or into a shoal, and certain shipwreck.

That is because "fate" is a marvelous acronym for "From All Thoughts Everywhere." And that includes all of your *own* previous thoughts, as well as all of the thoughts of others. First will come your own.

The first thing that will happen is that your personal creative Self will turn for direction to your own most powerful thought—which is often found in your subconscious. That is, you are not consciously aware of it. You will then produce an outcome. You simply won't do it consciously. You'll do it unconsciously, then claim that what happened was "fate," or "God's will."

In addition to your own thought, your future will also be impacted by the collective consciousness of the world around you; that is, the other human beings who people your life, with whom you travel on your journey, and, to some degree, all the people of the earth, whose combined attitudes too often create the collective experience of the lot of us.

Now, since many of the thoughts belonging to these other people may be strikingly different from each other, you may find yourself battered a bit. This will manifest itself as your feeling "torn" over what to do.

In life, indecision only breeds more indecision—and then, ultimately, a decision that is made *for* you. That is because, as you will soon discover, *not to decide is to decide.* The fact is, you are always deciding, it is just a matter of how you are doing it. You are always creating. It is merely a question of what method you use.

My recommendation: make a conscious personal choice about everything.

If you leave the choices about where the world at large is headed to the world at large, the collective consciousness of humanity will set the course and direction of your planet's future. You can either follow the collective consciousness, or help direct it.

If you are looking to *God* for direction in all this, you may want to consider the powerful questions raised here. What if your will for you is God's will for you? And what if the same is true for the collective will of humanity? What if God will *empower* humanity's collective will, but *will not alter it?*

Think about this.

This idea has enormous implications.

Perhaps "God" does not want something *from* humans, but exists only to give something *to* humans. And perhaps what God wants to give *to* humans is *exactly what humans want.* Nothing more, and nothing less.

Wouldn't *that* be interesting. . . .

Now please consider an additional possibility. This is a thought that could change everything for you, open up everything for you. This is a thought that could produce, inside you, instant peace, could bring you instant understanding, could offer you instant expansion of your consciousness and of your ability to live your own personal life in a way that finally makes sense to your soul. . . .

Consider the possibility that what you call "God" might also be called, simply, "life." Consider the possibility that God not only *created* life, but that God *is* life—and that *life is God, made manifest*.

This is not a new idea. You've probably heard this idea before, but have you ever seriously considered it? Have you ever thought deeply about its implications? For most people the answer to that question will likely be no, simply because it has not been permissible for this idea to be widely taught.

It has not been widely taught because it does not serve the Top Down, Power Over paradigm created by the earliest power structures of humanity, religion not the least among them.

This Top Down, Power Over paradigm was in evidence everywhere religion was found. One of humanity's earliest spiritual authority figures in modern times was the pope, who was said to have received his power, authority, and not incidentally, *infallibility* directly from God.

A king of England, furious at having to answer to the pope (who would not approve the king's decision to divorce one woman and marry another), simply started his *own* religion and proclaimed himself to be answerable only to the Most High.

The emperor of Japan was widely accepted in that country to be God Incarnate.

Entire races and nations have co-opted the Top Down, Power Over authority of God in order to render themselves somehow more elevated, more special, more *separate* from the rest of humanity. They called themselves the Chosen People, or One Nation under God, or the Nation of Islam.

Some people have sought to legitimize their worst deeds against those outside their separate and special group by saying that their actions were part of a *jihad,* or a *crusade*—a holy struggle *on God's behalf.*

Now if God wants nothing, *where does all this stand?*

16.

If God is not the highest point in a pyramid that passes authority down the line but is, rather, *the power that exists in the whole line,* and is therefore, in a sense, *the line itself,* what does that do to the Top Down, Power Over structures upon which so much of human society is built?

It disrupts them, that's what. It denies them their borrowed authority.

For this reason, powerful people and organizations, religions not the least among them, are not likely to encourage the teaching of a God who is One with Everything—a "Power With" rather than a "Power Over" kind of God.

If the words "God" and "life" *are* interchangeable, the implications are—if it's possible to imagine this—more than enormous. They're staggering, earthshaking, paradigm-shattering. This is because everyone knows what is true about life. Everyone may not know what is true about God, but everyone knows what is true about life.

What is true about life is that nothing stands outside life. Nothing exists without life, and life does not exist if nothing exists.

You are the expression of life itself. So is everything around you. Even so-called inanimate objects are found, when examined under a microscope, to consist of particles constantly in motion. These particles and their movements are all part of *life*. Indeed, everything in the observable universe is life, in some form.

The existence of life is confirmed by life itself. Life is self-referencing, self-confirming, self-sustaining, and self-evident. Life is the *evidence* of the existence of life.

Not only does everyone know these things, everyone agrees with these things. What makes what is being said here so dangerous is what happens when the word "God" is inserted where the word "life" appears. That produces this result:

Nothing stands outside God. Nothing exists without God, and God does not exist if nothing exists.

You are the expression of God Itself. So is everything around you. Even so-called inanimate objects are found, when examined under a microscope, to consist of particles constantly in motion. These particles and their movements are all part of God. Indeed, everything in the observable universe is God, in some form.

The existence of God is confirmed by God Itself. God is self-referencing, self-confirming, self-sustaining, and self-evident. God is the *evidence* of the existence of God.

Do you see the problem now? Those three paragraphs cause all the paragraphs in all the other books about God to fall apart. Everything crumbles. Not just a few of our beliefs about God, but the very basis upon which we have built so much of human society. It all comes tumbling down.

The wonderful thing about this, the exciting thing, is that we get to re-create ourselves anew, and rebuild our human society—and that is exactly what is going on right now. Humanity is in the process of rebuilding itself, and a natural part of that process calls upon humanity to take itself apart until enough of the disassembled pieces are lying before us that we can see how they might fit together in a new way. It's all part of the process of evolution.

A huge part of that process is our renewed exploration of this whole idea of God, and of our thoughts about *What God Wants*. If in fact the words "God" and "life" are describing the same thing . . . well, we have some major, *major* theological implications here.

Do we need more evidence of the existence of life than life itself? No. And what does *life* want? Nothing. Life simply is.

Life is an energy, a power, to be used. And it *is* being used, freely, by all. It has no expectations, no desires, no demands, no requirements, no need to be worshipped, and no need to punish those who fail to worship it. Life is a singular and unemotional reality. Life is the creator, and it's that which has been created.

Life is the source of life, and it's That Which Has Been Sourced. Life produces life, and life informs life about life through the process of life itself.

Life is, in a few words, the Alpha and the Omega, the All in All. There is nothing that IS that It is not.

If this is not the definition of God, then what is?

17

God *is* life, and life *is* God. Nothing stands outside God, and therefore there is no separation between God and anything at all.

Humanity's understanding of this will mark the End of Separation. That, in turn, will conclude the cycle that began when Separation was first taught.

The world's three largest religions are based on consecutive revelations, spanning thousands of years. Paraphrasing Huston Smith from his masterful book *The World's Religions,* we learn that . . .

I.   Abraham brought to humanity the revelation that there was not a string of deities ruling the sun and the stars and the weather and the crops and the land and the sea, but only one Ruler, one God, and Moses brought to humanity the revelation of what the One Ruler's rules were. He said there were ten of them.

2. Jesus brought to humanity the revelation that the One Ruler's rules could be reduced to One Rule—which has been called Golden.

3. Muhammad brought to humanity the revelation that the One Ruler's One Rule could be applied in very practical ways in everyday life, overlaying structure and procedure on a very broad guideline, converting generalities to specifics.

Now comes a new revelation. Not from one teacher but from many, not from one voice but from a chorus. That chorus is singing a different tune. It's the song of the soul.

4. The One Ruler's One Rule is Self-Rule.

This is the antithesis of everything that the world's largest religions teach. It's the thought that traditional religion says will be the cause of humanity's downfall. Wouldn't it be interesting if it turned out to be the thought that saved humanity?

There are those who say that putting oneself in the role of self-ruler—that is, in the role of God—is the worst insult to God. It's aggrandizement. It's ego run amok. It's the highest arrogance and the lowest blow. Human beings are *not* to attempt to rule themselves, but are to submit to God's rule. That is the preeminent doctrine of the major faiths, whatever else their differences might be.

And so, this new revelation comes as a shock. It feels like a theological convulsion. Believers in almost any kind of God are repelled. Yet it is important for thinking people to ask, What if it *were* true? What if God gave humans the power and the authority to rule over themselves, without any other power above them? What if *this* is what was meant by Free Will?

If the words "God" and "life" *are* interchangeable, if this is not simply an interesting thought but the truth, then the greatest mystery of all time—*who or what is God?*—would finally be solved.

Even traditional religion says that God is the All in All. If that is true, then there is nothing that exists except God, in Its varying Forms. God cannot be separated from God, and so is separate from nothing at all. God can differentiate Itself in countless ways, which It does as a means of Self-Expression, through which It becomes Self-Conscious. Yet differentiation is not division. Separation does not exist.

Given this reality, all that you could possibly give God, God already has received from you, because God IS you, doing the giving and the receiving. Therefore, God wants nothing from you, needs nothing from you, demands nothing from the individuated aspect of Itself that you think of as "you."

Likewise, all that God could possibly give you, God has already given you. It exists in you, *as* you. Therefore, you want for nothing. You need ask God for nothing. For it IS as it has been written: *"Even before you ask, I will have answered."*

If this is true, the only prayer to ever say is a prayer of gratitude. And that is, in fact, *the only prayer that any master has ever uttered.*

Here is the most powerful prayer I know of. I use it often. "Thank you, God, for helping me to understand that this problem has already been solved for me."

There are prayers of gratitude, and there are prayers of supplication. Masters know—and now it's time for you to know—that a prayer of supplication simply denies the truth. By asking for something, you are announcing that you do not now have it. This makes it very difficult for you to experience it, because you cannot experience what you deny.

All that you could need from God is now in you.

Do you feel you need more love? That is now in you.

Do you feel you need more compassion? That is now in you.

Do you feel you need more patience, understanding, kindness, mercy, forgiveness? That is now in you.

Once you know this, you'll never feel a need for these things again. All you'll feel is a desire to call them forth. Desire replaces need in the experience of the master.

Desires and needs are not the same thing (although many of us have made them so in our lives). To have a desire for something is not at all the same as having a need for it.

A desire is a preference. A need is a requirement. You can know whether you think you have a need for something or a desire for it by watching the amount of happiness you feel ebbing from you if you do not get it.

You would *prefer* to have chocolate ice cream, but it's okay to have vanilla. It's also okay to have none at all. You would *prefer* to have a lover with dark brown hair, but blond hair is all right, too. You would *prefer* to have no pain or reduced function in your body, but it's okay to have some. You can live with it. You can even be happy under such circumstances.

The human potential writer Ken Keyes Jr. proposed in his million-selling book *Handbook to Higher Consciousness* that if you feel your happiness is at stake in any given situation, you have probably created an addiction to a particular condition or circumstance. The key to inner peace, he said, is to elevate one's addictions from addictions to preferences.

This is the first step on the road to mastery. Each

moment is a step along that road. Each moment is a process. Have you ever thought about it that way? Each moment in life *is a process.* It is in the moment-to-moment of your life that you decide who you are and who you choose to be. And you do *not* have to be who you *used* to be. That is the great liberation. That is the great miracle. That is the great victory.

Yet you cannot win that victory if you think that you are fighting Someone Else's battle. If you imagine that you are fighting God's battle with Satan, that you are God's front line against the Devil, and that it is up to you to give God *What God Wants* in spite of the Devil's every attempt to get you to do otherwise, you will be caught up in the Great War That Cannot Be Won. It cannot be won because it does not exist.

What does God want? Nothing. Who is God's opponent? *No one.*

While God has no needs, God does have desires. Desire is the beginning of all creation. It is first thought. It is a grand feeling within the soul. And what is God's desire? If God were here now, talking to us today, I believe God would say:

"I desire first to know and experience Myself, in all My glory. Second, I desire that you shall know and experience Who You Really Are, through the power I have given you to create and experience yourself in whatever way you choose. Third, I desire for the whole life process to be an experience of constant joy, continuous creation, never-ending expansion, and total fulfillment in each moment of now.

"I have established a perfect system whereby these desires may be realized. They are being realized now, in this very moment. The only difference between you and Me is that I know this. In the moment of your own Total Knowing (which moment could come upon you at any time), you, too, will feel as I do always: totally joyful, loving, accepting, blessing, and grateful.

"These are the five attitudes of Godliness. You will notice that there is nothing said about being fearful, angry, violent, judgmental, or condemning. These are not attitudes of Godliness, although others have told you that they are. You are free now to let go of these ideas. You have always been free to do so. I want nothing from you, least of all your forced allegiance or your demanded love."

Here is God's greatest gift! If God wanted something, you would have to spend your whole life trying to figure out what it is, and then trying to give it to Him. Yet if God wants nothing, then you have total freedom to create the life you wish to experience.

That is, in fact, the definition of perfect love, in two words. Total freedom. It is also another definition of God. For God is the essence of total freedom. It is also a

description of the soul. Your soul is the expression of total freedom. The pity is that most humans believe just the opposite.

Most humans believe that the soul is "imprisoned" in the body, that it is in some kind of temporary holding place, or some sort of "school," where tragedy and suffering and learning the hard way are the order of the day. Indeed, many religions teach us some version of this. But those teachings are mistaken. They are erroneous. They run precisely counter to the true nature of things.

The essence of life and God and love and YOU is *freedom!*

You are free to call forth any reality that you wish. And the fastest way to call anything forth is to give it to another. You cannot give to another something that you do not have, yet it is the giving of it that produces the having of it. Now isn't that a wonderfully simple formula?

Let me use an example to provide a little more clarity on this. Let's say that what you seek is the experience of abundance. You can have that experience even if all you have in the world is a dollar.

The experience of abundance is yours the moment you find someone who has even less and then give to that person a portion of what you have. And this is where the rest of the world comes in. Here's how the new idea that will change your inner world will change your outer world. This is how the belief in a God without separation can create a society where people, like God, want nothing.

If it's true that the fastest way to experience that you have something is to give it away, then if you want to experience having something, you'll immediately *cause another to experience having it.* This works with everything in life, not just money. It works especially well with love.

If you want to experience that you have power, cause another to experience that they have power. If you want to experience compassion in your life, cause another to experience compassion in theirs. If you want to experience that you have more companionship, cause another to be companioned. If you want more humor in your life, bring more humor to the life of another. Try it with anything! Try it with everything! *It works.*

This teaching can be summed up in three words: BE THE SOURCE. For some this is a role reversal of enormous magnitude. Most people place themselves in the role of recipient of life's gifts. First they play the *supplicant,* then the *recipient.* First they ask, then they wait to receive. What I am saying here is that you should neither ask nor wait to receive. You should *give* what you wish to receive. That which *you* wish to experience, cause *another* to experience.

This simple message has been delivered before by others. One of those others said it in a way that has never been forgotten: "Do unto others as you would have it done unto you."

Humans are encouraged to do this not because this is a good and noble way to act, but because *this is how the universe works.* This is the *mechanism.* This is the *process.* What you do unto others IS being done unto you, because there is no one else BUT you, in differentiated form.

Now you see how a Theology of Oneness can create lack of want. Not just with God, but in the experience of that part of God known as human beings. If all of us saw ourselves as One, it would create a new ethic for our species and a new way of life on our planet. Virtually all of our behaviors would change.

What I know is that for behaviors to change, another change will have to take place first: A change in the basic way that we understand God. An enlargement and an expansion of the theologies of humanity.

A new kind of spirituality will have to be born. A spirituality built around two new and totally reconstructive core concepts: God wants nothing at all/God is separate from nothing at all.

These two concepts—because they *are* so new—will be repeated throughout the remainder of this text, in one form or another. Please do not think that this is inadvertent redundancy. It occurs very purposefully. When someone asks, "So, what is this new spirituality all about?" the answer will be on the tip of your tongue. Even if you don't agree with it, you'll know exactly what it's about, and be able to articulate that, whether you are for or against it. You'll be able to say that the New Spirituality is a spirituality that speaks not of *What God Wants,* but of *What God Is.*

18.

There is only one God. Whatever we think God is, most of the major religions of the world agree: there is only One of That.

Islam says it succinctly. "There is no god but God" *(La ilaha illa 'llah)*. Judaism and Christianity put it this way: "I am the Lord, thy God. Thou shalt not have false gods before me."

From "There is only one God" to "There is only One Thing at all" is a small shift. It's not a rejection of doctrine, but an enlargement. It's not an abandonment of traditional religious teaching, but an expansion.

This is important to understand. Our creation of a New Spirituality does not begin with us abandoning our faith tradition. This is not about rejecting religion. It is, in fact, about reinvigorating it, enlivening it, refreshing it.

Jesus was crucified for suggesting this. He wasn't saying to the world, Abandon your faith tradition. He was saying, There may be something more to know about all this. Others before and since have met with equally un-enthusiastic reception to such ideas. Yet Life Itself calls upon us to edge forward, move forward, *push* forward the limit of human understanding, to set the stage for the next great quantum leap, and to never, ever fall back.

Evolution is an upward journey, not a downward spiral.

It is time now for humanity's religions to grow. Growth is not death, but the opposite. So no one need worry that new spiritual ideas are going to kill off religions. They are not. They're going to *reinvigorate them*.

Religions now have an opportunity to shift from "There is only one God" to "There is only One Thing at all." This is a shift that some spiritual movements, such as the Sufi movement within Islam, have already made. Again it is Huston Smith who tells us that in Sufism the declaration *There is no god but God* was long ago changed to *There is nothing but God*.

I'll admit that to some, this idea may be worrisome. If there is Only One Thing That Is, then everything and everyone must be part of that One Thing—which means that the sense of having *someone else to go to* in moments of stress and times of trouble would be lost.

Where would one receive comfort, courage, wisdom, and strength? Where would one go for answers? To whom would one plead for a desired outcome? To whom could one complain . . . and know that the complaint was received with gentleness and love?

The happy news is that everyone can still go to God for all of these reasons. Just because God is everything doesn't mean that God has to stop being any part of what God always was. It means that God now gets to be even more—or more correctly, that you get to experience even more of God.

People can still go to God for comfort or wisdom. They can still ask God for what they need. Or they can thank God in advance for what they are about to receive. And they can complain to God as loudly as they ever did. They can question God, and they can even argue with God. They can now do this without fear, in the tradition of Abraham and Moses, in the tradition of Jesus, in the tradition of Muhammad, and of all the great masters who have truly understood God. For how do you truly understand God without questioning a little, arguing a little?

Is it possible for "regular people" to understand God, and to know *What God Wants?* You bet it is. You do not have to be an Ascended Master or a Living Saint in order to do this. Regular, ordinary, everyday people can do it. You can do it, and so can I. You're taking a big step in doing it right now.

There are those who don't want you to think that you can do it. They will tell you that even *attempting* to do it is a blasphemy. But that is inaccurate. That is simply not true. God would not create a world He did not want us to understand, a life He did not want us to comprehend, or an experience of Divinity He did not want us ever to know. What would be the point of that?

You will be open to the possibility of truly understanding God the moment you close yourself to its impossibility.

Let go of the idea that a God who can't possibly be understood is *What God Wants.* If you can do that, your understanding of God will change forever. This is, by the way, going to happen for humanity. It is not a question of whether, it is a question of when.

The fact that humanity's understanding of God will change will not mean that anything has to change in the way humans approach God, however. What might change is the way God approaches humans. Or, more accurately, the way people *believe* that God does.

Currently, people believe that God approaches humans in the same way that humans approach God—generally with a shopping list. There are things that human beings want, and they ask God for them. There are things that God wants, and He asks humans for them.

It's a trade deal. You give me this, and I'll give you that. You don't give me what I want and I won't give you what you want. You want to get to Heaven, but you can't unless you give me what I want.

This is roughly how humanity has it set out. It's perhaps a simplistic way of saying it, but that's basically it.

The only thing is, that's not the way it is.

If God could send only one Message to the World, and He was told that He had to keep it to one sentence, I think I know what that sentence would be.

You've got me all wrong.

And if the world really believed that it was God speaking, that sentence would create a miracle, because it would throw the discussion about God and about *What God Wants* wide open again. A discussion that everyone thought was closed would be reengaged. That could only be good for humanity. Theology might even expand again, like every other body of knowledge.

The fastest way for humans to expand their theology is for humans to expand their mind. This process can begin by asking the two Basic Questions of Theology, and then following those questions with a daring *What if?*

1. Who and What is God?
2. What does God want, and why?

Now, *what if* the standard answers to those questions—the answers humanity has heard for centuries—were incomplete? *What if* they were inaccurate? *What if* who and what you thought God is, God is not? *What if* what you thought God wants, God does not?

You have been offered answers to the two Basic Questions of Theology here. You are invited now to carefully reconsider those answers.

1. God is life, and everything in life.
2. God wants nothing, because God has, and *is,* everything that God could possibly want.

It's Unity Theology that produces these answers. Separation Theology could never do so. What would prove extraordinarily beneficial right now would be a shift in humanity's thinking from the second to the first. Such a shift would produce an end to the outcomes that only separation could inspire.

If God is everything,
has everything, and
has created everything,
what is God without?

19.

The reason that humanity as a whole has not shifted to a theology of unity is that much of humanity has sincerely believed that this is not *What God Wants*.

All talk of human beings being one with God and one with each other has been labeled fluffy, "new age," or out of touch with reality. Some have even called it apostasy.

Everything that humanity has been taught about God says that God is separate from humanity. God *wants* to be separate, because humanity in its present form is not *worthy* of unity with God. That is the teaching. That is the message.

God is Perfect and humanity is imperfect, and the Perfect cannot be united with the imperfect. This is an integral part of most human theologies.

So the imperfect must find a way to be Perfect. Yet that way cannot be found, because perfection is impossible to achieve in human form. Some religions even teach that humans are *born* in a state of imperfection, and so there is that problem going in. Other faiths say that humans may be born without blemish, but the task is to *remain* without blemish. All religions agree that on the journey of life there are temptations to which human beings fall prey. And so perfection is pretty much out of reach for most.

Still, one must try. One must strive. And if one strives for perfection, God will reward that effort with a final act of Grace, rendering the imperfect Perfect Once Again. Then, reunion with God in Heaven can be achieved.

This is another simplification, yet it comes very close to summarizing the doctrine of most religions.

And so there appears to exist a dichotomy. God wants humans—indeed, has *caused* humans—to be separate from God. Yet God has given humans a "way back home" because *What God Wants* is for humans *not* to be separate from God.

Hmmmm.

Now the unaskable question must be asked.

IS this *What God Wants?*

And the answer is no.

This answer changes everything. With it, the forward edge of human thought takes on new sharpness, and cutting through confusion becomes possible once again.

God does not want Oneness, with humans or any-thing else. God IS Oneness, and God does not want what God is already experiencing.

Human beings claim they want Oneness with God and with other humans. Yet humanity cannot experience what humanity already has *if it denies that it has it.*

This is the answer to another mystery: Why has it been so hard for the world's people to experience One-ness with God, or with each other?

You cannot experience what you are unwilling to express. You cannot get to where you already are. By the very act of leaving, you deny that you have arrived at where you want to go. Given this belief, *you can never experi-ence being there.* Your life will become a constant journey. It will be a journey to nowhere. It will be an endless search. A search for what is already there.

Looking for your glasses when they are on top of your head, you'll not find what you are searching for. You'll only find what you are searching for when looking into a mirror.

So far, humanity has not been very good about look-ing into mirrors. Introspection is not humanity's long suit. Having read this far, you've proven yourself to be the exception.

Why have humans denied their Oneness? Because

humans have confused *oneness* with *sameness*. We have not understood that no two fingers are alike, even though all are on one hand.

Afraid of losing individuality, desperately fearful of disappearing their own identity, human beings have tenaciously clung to their illusion of separation from each other, from all things in life, and from God. Especially from God. For if humanity is *not* separate from God, not only do people fear losing their individual identity, oneness with Deity suggests a whole new way of acting, a whole new way of being, for which religions have left humans woefully unprepared.

Yet it is not necessary to prepare yourself to love. Love is what you are, and so, loving comes naturally to you. *Stopping* yourself from loving is what is hard. Love of everyone and everything in life comes easily when fear of anyone or anything disappears. And fear of anyone or anything disappears when you realize that you don't need anything from anyone or anything, because everything you thought you needed to get from something or someone outside of yourself is available within you.

Now the circle completes itself, and you are Whole. Now, all that you find within you, you can give to others, who may not yet know that they are Whole as well.

Showing another that they are lovable is the fastest way to assist them in finding wholeness, in finding the love that is within themselves. When you love others you quite literally *give people back to themselves.*

In the end, love and fear are the only feelings there are. Life brings you a constant stream of opportunities to choose between the two.

Love is the feeling you are after in every moment, because love is the ultimate expression of self, and self-expression is the reason you are here. Love comes in many forms, but in only one quantity. You cannot love in degrees, but you *can* love in different ways. Filial love is the love you feel for family. Agape is the love you feel for a friend. Eros is the love you feel for a romantic lover. In the end, however, it is all love, simply expressed in different form.

Yet now comes a deeper understanding of why we fear losing our individual identity. If individuality is lost, *who will there be to love?*

This is what we are afraid of losing, ultimately: the *ability to love.* Because losing the ability to love means losing the ability to be and to experience who you really are. This feels like the ultimate loss of self, because the self *is* love, and It knows it. Yet you never need fear the loss of self *or* love, because you and love are one, and even if everything else and everyone else was gone, you would be able to feel love. Perhaps more so.

It is no accident that most mystical experiences occur in solitude. It is no coincidence that oneness and aloneness are so often companions. Wouldn't it be interesting if, just as the word "already" is an English contraction for "all ready," the word "alone" turned out to be an early English contraction for "all one"?

Are you all ready for that, or did you know that already?

You and love cannot be separated in any way, for love is what God is, and you are not separate from God, nor were you ever, nor will you ever be.

This is so very difficult for so many people to believe, because religion today teaches exactly the opposite. It tells us we *have* been separated from God, and it fills us with the fear that we could be separated forever. Yet one day, religion will teach this no more. One day, very soon, all religions will speak of the unity of God and humanity, and, indeed, of the unity of all of life, as does the Unity Church founded by Charles and Myrtle Fillmore in 1889.

While it is a wonderful spiritual movement, that

church has never gained the size or status of the world's major religions. Why? Because the largest number of humans have *refused to give up their belief in separation.* Ironically, to this day, it is the idea of *separation* that holds the greatest attraction—and the greatest fear. And so we fear what we believe in. Yet the message in this book comes to tell you that separation does not, and cannot, exist. It is in no way an aspect of life. It is always an illusion. Always.

Life is a unified expression of the only thing there is: life itself—which may also be called God. Our constant yearning for union is the outward worldly expression of the innermost knowing of the soul: we are one with all things and with life itself, and we seek always to experience that. That's what you're doing day to day, hour to hour, moment to moment. You are doing this through the living of your life and the expression of the life within you and all the celebrations of life that bring you joy.

Whenever you do anything magnificent, whenever you rise to an occasion, overcome an obstacle, love more than you thought you ever could, you feel joy. This is what you are looking for, this is what you are seeking always, because joy is love is life is God, *and you sense this* at the deepest level of your being.

You are looking for God, and God is right on top of

you. Yet if you do not know this, you will search in vain. Ultimately you will find the fullest measure of what you are looking for only when looking into a mirror.

This book is a mirror in written form. You placed this book before you, so that you might look at yourself.

Look, then, deeply. This book is speaking right to you.

20.

Reflecting on the human experience, it may be difficult to imagine a "wantless" God. We've been so trained, so indoctrinated, to believe that there is something God wants from us that it's almost impossible to conceive of a God who wants nothing. Yet consider the possibility that there is nothing that God *could* want, because there is nothing that God is not.

If God is everything, has everything, can create everything, and has created everything, what is God without?

If God is the All in All, the Alpha and the Omega, the Beginning and the End, the Unmoved Mover, the Omnipotent, Omniscient, Omnipresent, the Most Holy and the Most High, what is there left for God to want or need?

The answer keeps coming up, *nothing*. No matter which way you look at it, no matter how you try to twist it or turn it around, the answer keeps coming up, *nothing*.

This is the truth about God that cannot be believed. This is the truth about God that has not been taught.

Once again I invite you to consider this truth. Ponder deeply its implications:

GOD WANTS NOTHING.

This truth has not been taught because teaching this truth would change the world. Only the idea of a God who is *not* everything, and who is *separate* from what He is not, could justify or explain the world that humanity has created.

If the world as it presently exists is the world that people wish to support, if it's a world that they do not wish to see changed, they'll never condone the teaching of the idea of a God who is unified with everything, separate from nothing, and who needs nothing. Indeed, they'll fight this idea to the end, because they know that their world, and the power they have accumulated within it, *will come to an end anyway* should a new idea of a Unified, Complete God ever be embraced.

And so, from the earliest days of the young lives of all of your offspring, you'll be encouraged to teach of a God of Separation, a God of "wants," who must be placated, appeased, mollified, and obeyed.

You'll be asked to tell wide-eyed children of a God who has *not* been pleased by humans, because humans have disobeyed Him, and of a God who has distanced Himself from humans as a result.

You'll be invited to teach of a God who has thrown humans out of Paradise, forcing them to now earn their way back in.

Or, if you don't teach of original sin, you'll teach of the danger of living in sin, of living a life not reconciled with *What God Wants*—a God whose needs must be met, who *commands* that things be a certain way, or He will never allow humans to experience Oneness with Him.

Any story other than this—and certainly a story of a God who wants *nothing*—will be considered apostasy.

Yet if you changed your story, if you began telling of a God who wanted nothing because God is One with everything, including *humans,* and if you spoke gently and wisely with your children of all the ramifications of that, you could *change the human culture in one generation,* and that could *alter the human experience forever.*

The new culture would be a culture of oneness, of unity, replacing the culture of separation that now exists. In a culture of unity it would not only be *God* who wants nothing, it could be humans as well. Because the combined resources of all of humanity—which would be *made available* to all of humanity if humanity saw itself as

One—are more than sufficient to end human lack and suffering.

It's not going to be easy, though, for humanity to change its story, for that would mean accepting the fact that it may have made a huge mistake about God. Many human beings do not like to admit to having made any mistake, especially a mistake upon which their entire society is based. It seems easier to ignore the mistake than to recognize it and rebuild the society—*until the society is being so disassembled by the mistake itself that it needs to be rebuilt anyway.*

This is exactly what is happening right now.

Human society as we have known it is being slowly disassembled. It's being dismantled bit by bit right before our eyes. It's being done either by those who would seek to do us ill, or by those who would seek to *protect* us from those who would seek to do us ill. And it's being done unwittingly by the great mass of society that is simply settling, simply allowing what is happening to happen, and which is adding to the mix by shifting the values of our once common culture out of its own frustration, dismay, and despair.

Although we may not be able to feel that a great deal is different from one moment to the next, if we look back over a longer stretch of time, we see the impact of all this immediately. We know and admit that life as we knew it ten years ago no longer exists. Life as we knew it twenty years ago is a dream. And life as we knew it fifty years ago is a fantasy.

Walk down the street alone at night and feel perfectly safe? A fantasy. Move through the airport and get onto a plane without having to take off half your clothes? A fantasy. Swim in the river out back of town without worrying about pollutants? A fantasy. Put your full faith and trust in the big companies that are the backbone of your country? A fantasy. Watch television for a whole week without hearing about somebody being beheaded? A fantasy.

Looking into the face of this has not changed the assessment of most people regarding it. They see what they are looking at, but they do not look at what they are seeing. And so, even while their most fundamental beliefs about God and life are killing them, many humans still hold those beliefs to be the pathway to glory, peace, and happiness. Even while life is falling apart all around them, they do not see or admit what might be the cause.

The tendency of human beings to want to be right is what keeps the species from rapidly evolving. Humans have walked the earth for millions of years, and in that time many have barely evolved past their most primitive behaviors.

As we have been pointing out here, humanity still faces today the problems it has always faced. And those problems have grown, moving in *exactly the opposite direction* from that which one would expect of an evolving society. We don't need to get into any more numbers or statistics here, but let's just look at things generally. . . .

The problems of greed and avarice and abuse of power, the problems of poverty and hunger and disease, of the poor and the destitute, the hopeless and the helpless, the hungry and the starving, have not gone away. Those problems have increased, not decreased.

The problems of disenfranchisement and brewing anger created by the gap between the rich and the poor have not disappeared. In fact, human society has not closed that gap, it has widened it immensely.

The problems of violence and the wholesale killing of innocents have not abated. In fact, they have spread around the world—and across age groups as well. Now, even children are killing. Thirteen-year-olds are strapping on explosives to blow themselves up at checkpoints in the Gaza Strip. Seven-year-olds are pushing three-year-olds out of windows in Chicago.

We've talked a lot about all this now, so let this be our closing comment about the present state of things: The fact of the matter is that there is more suffering on the planet than a society that was truly civil would allow, permit, or tolerate—much less create. There is more lack than there is plenty, more fear than there is love, more unrest than there is peace, and more indifference than there is concern. If there were not more, these problems would go away.

To many, it seems very much as if humanity is not merely failing to make progress, it's actually falling behind. There are those who say we are *devolving*. Things are, they say, getting worse, not better, harder, not easier, and what passes for progress masquerades the truth of humanity's ineptitude.

The big joke is that it takes longer to get across our big cities in a car now than it did 150 years ago in a horse and buggy. It takes longer to get a package across the country by postal service than it did by pony express. *And it costs more.* Humanity is paying more and getting less, and it's calling this the good life.

But now humanity is paying with *life itself* for its lack of progress in understanding life itself, for it is life itself that is now being threatened, and in too many cases ended, because of that lack of understanding.

Humanity must now come to a new understanding of life, and of that which animates life, which we call Allah or Brahma or God or Yahweh or Jehovah or Lord or the many other names we have given to the Supreme Being and the Essence, the All and the Only. In this it's no longer a question of convenience, it's a question of survival.

If we have not made sufficient progress in our sociological development to keep up with our technological advancement, it may be because we still insist on using that model I spoke of earlier, of power OVER rather than power WITH, to build our societies. We're still using ownership and control of our resources, materials, products, and services, rather than sharing and accessibility, as our basic economic and social model. Soon that could be our democratic model as well.

Don't believe it? Get this. In the September 2004 elections in Hong Kong, one-half of its legislative body was elected by the "non-human vote."

The what?

I said, the Non-Human Vote.

You think I'm making this up? I couldn't make something like this up. Only a science-fiction writer like George Orwell or Robert Heinlein could make something like this up. I am not a science-fiction writer. I only tell the truth.

I am telling you that in Hong Kong there is now something called the Non-Human Vote. The government in Hong Kong allows *corporations to cast votes.* They and other special interest groups, such as educators, then place their own representatives in the legislative body, filling half the seats!

I was told by residents of Hong Kong during a visit there just after the city's last legislative election that this is justified by the fact that Hong Kong exists and has its being as a political entity only because of the success of its commercial enterprise. Hong Kong is arguably the most commercially and business-oriented place in the world, and because the companies that create its economy are so vital to this Special Administrative Region of China, those companies are given votes in its elections, and seats in its legislature!

How long do you think it will be before this concept of a Non-Human Vote spreads across the rest of the world? Want to take any bets?

The result of this fascinating, surrealistic, Future-World mechanism of self-rule is that self-rule does not exist at all, but has actually been taken from the people and given, now in more specific terms than ever before, to corporate giants. Before this it was simply assumed that large corporations *controlled* the votes. Now, they actually *get* the votes!

This would be like giving special interest groups in the United States half the seats and half the votes in Congress. (Of course, there are those who say that this is exactly what they get, only it's by proxy. Perhaps it would be a little more honest if we just gave them actual votes in our elections and seats in Congress right up front. I can hear the debates now. "Will the gentleman from Connecticut yield for a question from the gentleman from Enron?")

A system such as this means, of course, that fewer and fewer individual human beings around the world will be getting what they want. And when humans are not getting what they want, or when they feel threatened (by something real or imagined), they will use violence to resolve the problem.

It used to be that our violence could damage only a few. Then our technology advanced, and we learned to damage a great many. Now we can damage everyone.

It used to be that we employed violence as a last resort. Now, with full moral justification, we use it as a *first* resort. We call this "robbing from the rich and giving to the poor," or "righteous war," or "jihad," or "preemptive strike." Each of us has our name for it, and for each of us that name justifies our actions.

So this is where humanity is. This is just what is so. After all these years it still comes down to who can strike the most terror into the hearts of the most people. Everyone considers that they are "in the right" in doing what they are doing.

The fact is that too many human beings still see it as more important to be "right" than to be happy, and they have made that choice many times, individually and collectively. Many have done so because they fervently believe that righteousness is *What God Wants*. Yet what if they are not right *about that?*

21.

We can get out of this mess, and here's how. *We have to use the same method that got us into it.*

Humanity's collective reality—its cultural story, if you please—has been created over a period of many, many years through a three-step process. This process goes on to this very day. It looks like this:

1. People are given **information** about God and about *What God Wants* from their elders—information that they widely embrace as true.
2. This information sponsors **beliefs** about Life and how it is, as well as how it "should" be.
3. These beliefs produce **behaviors** within the human family that create humanity's on-the-ground experience.

Everything begins with the original information. Even those people who do not "believe in God" are affected by the ideas *about* God held by those who do. This is so because (a) there are many more people creating the common culture worldwide who do believe in some sort of God than who do not, and (b) all societies are built on laws and customs rooted in the sacred myths and cultural stories of the society's ancestors.

While everything begins with the original information, it is that very information that *too few have chosen to question*—even if the information is producing a disaster. We simply refuse to question our most basic assumptions and our most basic beliefs. Thus, humanity has for centuries tried to solve its problems at every level except the level at which the problems exist. It continues to do so today.

We approach our problems as if they were political problems, open to political solutions. We talk about them, we hold debates about them, we pass resolutions about them. When nothing changes, we seek to solve our problems through economic means. We throw money at them, or withhold money from them, as in the case of sanctions. When that fails, we say, Aha, this is a problem to give to the military. We'll solve it with force. So we drop bombs on it. That never works, either, if a long-term solution is what anyone is looking for, but do you think we would learn?

Naw. We just start the cycle all over again.

The reason we keep running and getting nowhere "like a mouse on a wheel" is that no one dares to look at the *cause* of the ongoing condition we seem fated to endure. Either we truly don't know, or we are afraid to admit, that our biggest problem today is not a political problem, it's not an economic problem, and it's not a military problem.

The problem facing humanity today is a spiritual problem.

Once this is understood, the solution becomes obvious. Until it's understood, the solution escapes everyone.

It's what people believe that creates their behavior. Therefore, it is at the level of belief, not at the level of behavior, where behavior can most profoundly be modified. For decades we've been talking in psychology circles about *behavior modification,* or Behavior Mod. What we really should be talking about is Belief Mod.

Ah, but here we go. Oh, boy. Watch out. We're talking now about the most sacred part of people's underpinnings. Many people would rather die for their beliefs—or kill others—than change them.

It doesn't matter whether the beliefs are functional. That is, whether they are working, in the sense of making people happy and producing a better life. Many people would rather be unhappy doing what they believe than happy doing something else. They are actually *happy* being *unhappy.* Under this convention, as I have already pointed out, suffering is a virtue.

What makes this unlikely scenario possible? It's quite simple. People will allow themselves to be unhappy, they will even kill themselves with bombs strapped to their chests or seated in the cockpit of airliners, if they think they are doing *What God Wants.*

They do think that, of course, and they are part of a large number of people in our world who hold an inaccurate belief about God.

Part of the problem that exists at the level of belief—and this is something that no one wants to say out loud, but that must be said—is that *the world thinks that God condones violence as a means of conflict resolution.*

Indeed, it is from the written accounts in the Bible, in the Qur'an, in the Bhagavad Gita, in the Book of Mormon, and in other scriptures, that many people of many faiths draw the moral authority for their actions, and that every schoolchild of every culture learns about the Wrath of God.

Of course, there is no such thing as the Wrath of God. It's one of humanity's false beliefs. But many humans think that there *is* such a thing. They also think that it's appropriate for us to act with each other in the same way that God acts with us. After all, *if we can't use God as our model, who can we use?*

22.

A world in which we perpetrate violence upon each other would not even be possible if human beings changed their most fundamental belief about God, about life, and about each other, and that is the point being made over and over here. We insist on believing that we are separate from God and that we are separate from each other and that life is about living in separation.

It is our Separation Theology that has created the world as it is today: a place strikingly lacking in peace— and in the ability to create it. Not only between people, but in the human heart. That, of course, is where peace must start first; that is where it must be born. Behavior is the child of belief, and belief is held closely in the heart. When we believe in our heart that We Are All One, everything will change. *Everything.*

What we have to do, our challenge here, is to find a way to get people to act collectively as they almost always do individually. Individually, we almost always act in the best interests of those we love. The only question remaining, then, is, *who do we love?* Our challenge, in a nutshell, is *group consciousness.*

Thus far we haven't seemed to be able to get our act together at this level. Oh, we've made efforts, for sure. We've formed associations and alliances and leagues and consortiums and have tried our best to unite the nations behind ideas that no one could possibly object to, such as ending world hunger. But we can't do it. We can't even do that. We can't even stop people from starving to death on a planet where there's more than enough food for everyone.

And why? *Why?*

The answer is the same as it was before. *Because we keep trying to solve our problems at every level except the level at which the problems exist.*

To use this specific example, we keep saying that getting enough food to people is a political problem, but it's not. We keep pretending that it's an economic problem, but it's not. We have even tried to frame it in some areas of the world as a military problem. It is not. We've got to keep saying this over and over again until we get it. *It's a spiritual problem.* Not just world hunger, but *all* the major problems we face. They are created by what we believe.

The simple fact is that we have not been taught that we *are all members of a single group called Humanity.* Or we may have been taught that, but we have not been taught what that *means* as a practical matter, nor encouraged by any of humanity's institutions to take what it means and place that into our daily lives in any truly functional way. And so it's just a bunch of words.

Those people are massacred in Darfur, and we *tsk·tsk* and shake our head and wonder what the world is coming to. Would we let one member *of our own family* die of starvation or genocide? Of course not. We would do anything to stop it. So the problem is clear. *We don't see the people in Darfur as members of our own family.*

Yet we *do* see other people as members of our own family when it is not members of our own family who are hurting them. Consider humanity's response to the magnitude 9.0 earthquake on December 26, 2004, off the coast of the Indonesian island of Sumatra. More than 175,000 lives were claimed by the tsunami that quake generated, with nearly two million left homeless, but in its aftermath we mobilized ourselves rapidly, raising huge sums of money overnight, bringing food and medical supplies to the hungry and the injured, doing what we could as fast as we could to alleviate the suffering.

What made Darfur, where over 75,000 died from disease, hunger, and violence, and where two million were left hungry and homeless, any less worthy of such a response? Could it be that when humans are damaging one another, we see ourselves as separate as a guilt-management device?

Whatever the reason we have adopted it, our Separation Theology has separated humanity from *itself*—and, indeed, from all of life. Because we believe that God is a separate entity, we believe that life is something that is happening TO us, not THROUGH us. We look at something like Darfur, or the 2004 tsunami, and *we don't see at any level how we are causing this to happen.*

Our *consciousness* is what is causing it to happen. Our *consciousness of separation* is what allows it to occur. On reflection, our connection to the Darfur experience is easy to grasp—if not so easy to admit. In the instance of the tsunami, is it possible that all the years of underground testing of nuclear weapons—testing that has ripped earth's interior apart and left gaping holes beneath its surface—has added to the shifting of the tectonic plates, advancing by millennia the drifting of those plates and their crashing into one another? Is it possible that the many other ways in which we mistreat our earth have produced any of the additional environmental disasters and challenges with which we have been increasingly confronted?

Do humanity's behaviors, decisions, and choices—

which arise out of our *consciousness*—have any impact at all on the ongoing process of the planet's evolution, and of life itself?

Looking at purely practical matters, is it possible that something as simple as a better tsunami warning system (or, in this case, *any* tsunami warning system) might have saved tens of thousands of lives in December 2004, and that such a system could have been put into place if humanity had seen itself as One and simply made it a priority? (Other, richer, nations and regions already have it.)

How can *not* having made it a priority be justified? How can richer nations not having freely shared their technology with poorer countries be rationalized? Well, of course, it can't. And so now, stricken by the horror of hundreds of thousands dead, and smacked in the face by their own conscience, governments of the world's well-to-do nations are rushing to make it possible for an early-warning system to be put in place elsewhere on the globe, as well as along their own shores. A bit late, perhaps, but a tardy sense of "we are all in this together" is, one supposes, better than no sense of it at all.

It's frustrating, isn't it? Even *reading* about it is frustrating, because it seems as if we're being beaten up over and over about problems we didn't create and about which there is nothing we can do.

But there IS something we can do. *That's the point.*

We can take an honest look once and for all at our most fundamental beliefs about God and about Life, and we can admit that many of them are no longer working. We can admit that many of them *never* worked. Then we can change them. Then we can help others change them. And by this means we can raise the consciousness of humanity.

We can do this! We *can*.

For thousands of years humans have asserted that God has an agenda separate from our own. This allows us to shift responsibility for our lives to Someone Else. Even more conveniently, people insist that they must serve God's agenda, then they give themselves permission to define that agenda as they wish. (Have you noticed certain figures on the world stage doing this?) And they do so, according to *their own beliefs* about God and about *What God Wants*.

A striking example of this is that two leaders can send people into war, each claiming to have God on their side.

If people used humanity's interests rather than what they claim to be God's interests to guide them in their actions, they might achieve remarkably different results. Humanity's interests cannot be so easily ill-defined. Humanity's interests, unlike God's, are self-apparent.

The greatest interest of humanity is *life*. This is the greatest interest of God as well, but some people claim otherwise. They imagine that God has a *greater* interest than human life—and that is what allows them to waste it with impunity. That is what allows them to fly airplanes into buildings shouting "Allah is great!" or drop bombs on the heads of innocent civilians, paid for with money on which is imprinted *In God We Trust*.

Yet the moral certitude that comes from so many of humanity's theological theories falls apart in the face of this three-word message: GOD WANTS NOTHING.

That's why this book is so dangerous.

23.

Now here's the most dangerous chapter of this book. You might have thought it was chapter 13, but this is the real zinger here. This is the part that some people of power don't want you to read, because they know you'll get all excited about it, and that'll be the beginning of the end of their game. We're going to take a look now at those same categories we explored earlier, only through the prism of our new understanding of *What God Wants*.

For centuries we have been seeking to create Peace on Earth, Goodwill to All. I believe that we may still be able to do that. Time is short, yes. We're running out of runway, yes. Our environment may not hold out the way we are treating it, and our technology—which is giving us the ability to use "dirty bombs" and other weapons of mass destruction, including chemical and biological weapons—is running way ahead of our spiritual development. Still, I remain optimistic. I think we can do it. I think we can make the Christmas card come true.

Now, there are two ways we can go about trying to achieve that. One way is the way that organized religions have been trying for centuries: convert everyone to the One True Religion and get them to follow the rules. This is the Save the World by Spreading the Faith approach that has not only failed to save the world, but has moved us closer to destroying it.

The other way is to expand human consciousness to include the awareness that God and life are One, that everything in life is part of a unified whole, and that our different religions are merely wonderfully divergent paths to the same destination—a destination the soul need not strain to reach, because it is already there: the everlasting embrace of God.

The doctrine of Oneness used as a basis for all human political, economic, social, educational, and religious decisions would breathtakingly alter life as it is lived on the earth. The biggest change would be a relinquishing of our belief that God wants something from us.

If people thought that God wanted nothing, fear and guilt would all but disappear from their spiritual lives. That would enrich the human race immensely. At last it could embrace a new kind of God, and that would cause people to live a new kind of life on an individual, personal level, as well as globally as part of the collective called humanity.

What kinds of changes might humanity see? What kinds of shifts could occur in your personal life? Let's take that second glance at the categories into which beliefs about life were divided before, and see how things might look different with a new thought about *What God Wants*.

God

Humans will understand that Adonai, Allah, Brahman, Elohim, God, Jehovah, Krishna, and Yahweh are among the many names humans have given to The One Thing That Is. They'll also understand that The One Thing That Is (abbreviated in English as TOTTI) is all that exists. There is nothing that is not part of The One Thing That Is.

TOTTI is the Supreme Being, the Creator of Heaven and Earth, the Giver of Life, Omnipotent, Omniscient, Omnipresent, and Wise beyond Human Understanding.

TOTTI is the Alpha and the Omega, the beginning and the end, the Unmoved Mover, not separate from humanity but one with it, not separate from life but one with it, both the Creator and the Created—with the Created necessarily then being in TOTTI's own image.

TOTTI wants and needs nothing. How could it? It's

the only thing that is. TOTTI does not, therefore, sit in Judgment of anyone, nor decide at some sort of Reckoning whether a Part of Itself will be able to rejoin the Whole of Itself, since no Part was ever separated from the Whole, and could not be.

One result of this new teaching: No human beings will be afraid of God, or Allah, or Yahweh, or TOTTI, or whatever name they choose to give to the All in All. They'll simply love God completely and utterly as the amazing amalgam that God is.

Humans also will no longer confuse love and fear. They'll see clearly that these are mutually exclusive, that they cannot both exist at the same time in the same space. The effort to pretend that they can, that they somehow go together, is what has turned many humans into neurotic beings, trying to live out a reality that is completely out of alignment with what they instinctively know to be so, and completely contrary to their nature.

God's Word and God's Messenger

Humans will understand that God's words are found in all of the world's Holy Scriptures, and that no scripture is more authoritative, more complete, more accurate, or more authentic than any other, but that each contains great wisdom and each leads to a greater understanding of The Only Truth There Is (TOTTI).

So, too, will humans understand that there are many messengers of TOTTI—indeed, that all people everywhere are messengers, and that their message is their life, lived. For life is a process by which life is informed about life through the expression of life itself. Life tells life about life through life. TOTTI is what it shows itself to be. Every human being is both the Messenger and the Message.

One result of this new teaching: Human beings will stop trying to figure out which is the right text and which is the right messenger and will simply look closely to see which text and which messenger speaks to them in a way that makes it possible for them to express and experience their connection to the Divine, and to understand the great mysteries and the great wonders of life. Humans will also stop trying to convince others that the messenger and the text that has touched their heart is the only one that people should turn to.

Wars and killing in the name of a particular text or messenger will be impossible to justify under these circumstances, and will all but disappear.

Heaven and Hell

Humans will understand that the Universe is not some outlying territory separate from Heaven, but that it's part of The Only Territory There Is (TOTTI). They'll come to understand that Heaven is the experience of traveling through that territory in a state of bliss—a state that may be reached at any time, no matter where within the territory of life one happens to be.

Humans will also understand that life is not a system of reward and punishment, and that no one is sent to Hell or condemned by God.

At least one major world religious leader, Pope John Paul II, has already clarified this. He made a theologically breathtaking statement before a papal audience in Rome on July 28, 1999.

"Damnation cannot be attributed to an initiative of God because in His merciful love He cannot want anything but the salvation of the beings He created," the pope declared to an astonished world. Eternal damnation is never the initiative of God, it's the self-imposed punishment of those who choose to refuse God's love and mercy, the pontiff added.

And what is this "damnation" that is referred to? Is it endless fiery torture in that place of flames called Hell? No, said the pope. Hell, he announced, does not exist as a place, but is "a *situation* in which one finds oneself after freely and definitively withdrawing from God, the source of life and joy."

The pope said people must be very careful in interpreting the biblical descriptions of Hell—"the inextinguishable fire" and "the burning oven"—which he said are symbolic and metaphorical. These picture phrases are meant to "indicate the complete frustration and vacuity of a life without God," John Paul said.

So what is the truth? Are any human beings in Hell? That is, Pope John Paul II said, "not something we can know."

This is a remarkable statement from the spiritual leader of one of the largest religious organizations in the world. Asked that question ten years ago, there are very few priests, ministers, rabbis, or mullahs on the planet who would have responded with anything other than an immediate and unequivocal *"Yes! What do you think we've been trying to tell you???"* But the pope has apparently had some new ideas on this subject that are very much in concert with the New Spirituality, because they eliminate the fear of Hell as a theological tool with which to construct an entire spiritual reality that has deeply affected humanity.

One result of this new teaching: People's concept of life will no longer be shaped by a win-lose construction of the Afterlife. They'll begin to formulate new ideas of what is experienced after death. Humans will then no longer structure their lives around the hope of getting to Heaven or the fear of going to Hell. They'll stop doing extraordinary, shocking, or self-destructive things to produce the first outcome. They'll find different reasons to act as they act, choose what they choose, say what they say, and think what they think. They'll create that *new measure of morality* for which the world has been searching.

Life

Humans will understand that life is not a school, neither is it a time of testing. If God wants nothing, there is no reason for a test. If humans are One with God, there is nothing to learn, there is only to remember what has been forgotten.

Humans will also understand that life is not an ordeal during which the soul struggles to get back to God, but rather is an ongoing process by which the soul seeks to grow, to expand, and to experience its intrinsic nature, which is unlimited and divine. It will also be clear that this process, called *evolution,* never ends, but is experienced by the soul everlastingly, at different levels and in different life forms.

Humans will also understand that life is not limited to what can be perceived by the five senses, but is far wider in scope and deeper in dimension than humans at first imagined or have ever been told by religion.

One result of this teaching: Much more attention will be paid to what is not perceived by the five senses, and this will be the basis of a new understanding of life and how it might be most joyfully and wonderfully experienced.

Life will not be lived with an eye toward the Afterlife, but with an eye toward what is being created, expressed, and experienced at many levels of perception in the Holy Moment of Now. Humans will become increasingly aware that "now" is The Only Time There Is (TOTTI).

Life will not be experienced as a struggle or as an effort to "get back home" to God, but rather as a free-flowing expression of one's intrinsic nature, which is unlimited and divine.

"Getting to heaven" will no longer be the ultimate purpose in life. *Creating* heaven wherever you are will be seen as the prime objective. To experience this, people will not have to confess any sins or fast during daylight hours or travel on pilgrimages or go to places of worship weekly or tithe regularly or perform any particular ritual or act—although they may choose to do any of these things if it pleases them, or helps to remind them of who they are in relationship to God, or assists them in staying connected with their purpose.

Because of their deeper understanding and rich personal experience of life as a unified field, for people everywhere life itself will become the prime value, and the core around which all spiritual understanding and expression revolves.

Male and Female

Humans will understand that God is not a male, nor is God a female, but that God has no gender at all.

Because the idea of God as a male being will be rejected as simplistic and inaccurate, humans will also understand that men are not superior to women in any way. The thought that God wants men and women to have limited roles in life will be abandoned in favor of a thought of complete equality for women and men. Indeed, with regard to all people everywhere, of whatever race, creed, gender, age, or sexual persuasion, the lack of superiority and the absolute equality of individuals will be The Only Thought There Is (TOTTI).

One result of this teaching: Discrimination and abuse of females will disappear from civil society.

Marriage

Humans will understand marriage to be a spiritual tool, a sacred device, used by evolving beings to play out their soul's agenda and to complete that part of their journey that involves mutuality with a particular Other for the purpose of growth and the continued re-creation of Self.

They'll also understand that all human relationships are hallowed ground, that intimate relationships with a significant other are highly impactful and important, and that holy matrimony is a contract of extraordinary meaning and consequence.

Humans will be aware that no two souls meet by chance, but every human encounter is purposeful and laden with gifts, and every melding of hearts and partnership of souls, however long or brief, is the playing out of a mystical agreement—God's Invitation to experience and expand in awareness, consciousness, understanding, and expression of the Divine Essence of Being.

One result of this teaching: People will not see marriage as an opportunity to complete themselves or to somehow bring to their lives "something that is missing," but to celebrate the fact that there is *nothing* missing, that they are Whole, Complete, and Perfect just as they are, and to expand and grow in their experience of this through the wondrous miracle of bonded relationship.

Humans will never again enter into marriages (or stay in them) for reasons of security, because they'll understand that the only real security is not in owning or possessing, nor in being owned or possessed . . . not in demanding or expecting, and not even in hoping, that what they think they need in life will be supplied by another . . . but rather, in knowing that everything they desire in life . . . all the love, all the wisdom, all the insight, all the power, all the knowledge, all the understanding, all the nurturing, all the compassion, and all the strength . . . resides within them. Which is God within

People will also not enter marriage in any way that would limit, control, hinder, or restrict their partners or themselves from any true expression and honest celebration of that which is the highest and best within them—including their love of God, their love of life, their love of people, their love of creativity, their love of work, and any aspect of their being that genuinely represents them and brings them joy.

Finally, people will not see marriage as producing obligations, but rather as providing opportunities . . . opportunities for growth, for full self-expression, for lifting their lives to the highest potential, for healing every false thought or small idea they ever had about themselves, and for ultimate reunion with God through the communion of two souls.

They'll see marriage as truly a Holy Communion . . . not an everlasting union between a man and a woman, for better or for worse, but a union between two loving people lasting as long as both people choose to be united, a journey through life with one's beloved as an equal partner, sharing equally both the authority and the responsibilities inherent in any partnership, bearing equally what burdens there be, basking equally in the glories. Humans will understand that the success of a marriage is measured by what has been given and received, understood and remembered, shared and healed, and by what growth has been produced.

And finally, all humans will understand that marriage is about teamwork, the teamwork of two souls who have created a holy team to do the holy work of life itself, which is the work of growth and the expression of divinity through the experience of unity. Those who have a truly holy union will know that their union is a *three-way union,* that their team consists of each other and of God, and that this is The Only Team There Is (TOTTI).

Sex

Humans will understand that sexual union is a glorious and wonderful expression of the Oneness of Being, an extraordinarily powerful and deeply meaningful experience of the most intimate physical, emotional, psychological, and spiritual aspects of the self that two people can share, and a celebration of love and life that has no equal in physical form.

They'll also see clearly that sex is not laden with any taboos, do's or don'ts, but is meant to be experienced joyfully by two consenting adults in whatever way brings pleasure and respects the boundaries, desires, and agreements of both.

Humans will also understand that the human body is sacred, not embarrassing, and that no part of the body is anything other than totally beautiful, and all of the body may therefore be shown and seen without shame.

One result of this teaching: Sexual guilt and sexual shame will virtually disappear from the human family. So will sexual assault. Sexual expression will be lifted to the level of the profound, never lowered to the level of the profane, and there will be no thought that spiritual energy and sexual energy do not mix, but rather, it will be taught that sexual energy is a beautiful expression of spiritual energy in physical form.

Many more people will become familiar with tantric sex, in which the sexual experience is expressed as sacred union. *Tantra* is defined as "the realization of the Oneness of the Self and the visible world," and when sex is experienced as sacred, it is, in physical form, The Only Tantra There Is (TOTTI).

Homosexuality

Humans will understand that there is no form and no manner in which the expression of a love that is pure and true is inappropriate.

One result of this teaching: Humans for whom same-gender sexual attraction feels most natural will no longer be denounced, vilified, condemned, ostracized, isolated, assaulted, and killed by people who believe they are doing God's will. Their wholesale oppression will end.

Love

Humans will understand that love is neither quantifiable nor conditional. They'll know that the term "conditional love" is an oxymoron, and that love cannot be parceled out in units of varying size, but is either present or not present, in any given moment and with any given person, as an experience of the Whole Heart and Mind and Soul—a full expression of the Blessed Essence of Being Itself.

While humans will understand that love cannot be quantified, they'll see that it can be expressed in different ways, and that these different *kinds* of love are what they confused with different *levels* of love in the past.

Because it will be clear that <u>God wants nothing from human beings and gives everything *to* human beings. God will be the ultimate model</u>, at <u>last, of what love is and</u> means.

One result of this teaching: The veil of confusion around love will lift at last. Humans will use the term "love" to mean an entirely different thing than it now means in most human relationships. It will never again be confused or used interchangeably with the word "need." The term "love" will be deeply respected, as it will be clear that it carries actual energy (as do all words, but this one to a very high degree) and produces more different and powerful vibrations than perhaps any other term in humanity's many languages, except the various names of Deity.

Indeed, it will be very clear that there is no universal term, common to all languages, that comes closer to capturing the very Essence of God. <u>Humans will see clearly that to define God in one word, "love" is The Only Term There Is (TOTTI)</u>.

Free Will

Humans will understand that their will is truly *free*. They'll know that God will never cause them to suffer dire consequences in the Afterlife for making one choice over another in life.

One result of this teaching: The contradictions will be taken out of God's promise to humans, and this will inspire humans to remove the contradictions from their own promises to each other. A new definition of "freedom" will be created, one that reflects what the word was always intended to mean—the complete and total lack of limitations of any kind.

Suffering

Humans will understand that God does not want anyone to suffer, ever, and certainly does not require any being to suffer needlessly or endlessly in order to "stay in good standing" with God, or do "what is right."

One result of this teaching: If they have any control over the circumstances, people will no longer require themselves or others to endure ongoing physical pain needlessly or endlessly. People will also understand the difference between suffering and pain, observing that pain is an objective experience, while suffering is a subjective decision about it.

Many mothers experience the pain of childbirth not as suffering at all, but as an intense but joyous celebration of life itself, *producing* life itself, through the *process* of life itself. Rising to this level of awareness about all pain is a matter of elevating one's consciousness and adopting a change of perspective, which can alter an entire experience. Thus, *Consciousness* is used as a transformative tool, creating in the human mind an experience of the body that defies exterior evidence—and transmutes it.

Money

Humans will understand that money is an energy like any other form of energy, that it has neutral value in and of itself, and that it's what one does with money that gives it value. They'll also understand that God has nothing against money, and that the idea that money and spirituality do not mix is false.

One result of this teaching: People will be freed of the guilt around money, and society in general will change its attitude about money, making it possible for persons who do good things for the world—even for those who do

"God's work"—to earn as much money as they can or wish without being made wrong.

It will become clear that for society to become maximally functional, the highest reward might most beneficially be given to persons bringing society the highest value—not the other way around.

Morality

Humans will understand that morality is not unchanging, nor is it dictated by *What God Wants,* since God wants nothing at all.

One result of this teaching: People will begin to take the question of defining morality firmly into their own hands, refusing to cede authority to any organization or institution. The outcome of this will be that contemporary morals will more authentically reflect contemporary behaviors. Humans will thus be able to act the way they have routinely acted, only doing so without guilt or fear of being judged, "outed," or condemned.

The argument that humanity's values will drop should this occur will not be validated, because people, given higher levels of responsibility for themselves, will be found to rise to higher levels of greatness in the creation and expression of who they are.

This is the purpose and the wonder of life, they'll see: *To constantly re-create ourselves anew in the next grandest version of the greatest vision we ever held about Who We Are—as a species, as individuals, and as divine beings in a causal universe.*

Death

Humans will understand that death does not exist. They will know that our opportunity to learn and to grow is never over, and that the time to be rewarded or punished for how we lived our lives will never come, because life is not a reward-and-punishment proposition but rather a process of continuous and unending growth, expansion, self-expression, self-creation, and self-fulfillment.

Death will be understood to be simply and only a transition—a glorious shifting in the experience of the soul, a change in our level of consciousness, a freedom-giving, pain-releasing, awareness-expanding breakthrough in the eternal process of evolution.

One result of this teaching: Many humans will know that death is not something to be feared, but a wonderful part of the wonderful experience called Life Itself.

People will talk about death freely and without undue sadness. People will not feel compelled to cling to life when they are suffering and dying, because they'll know that there is nothing BUT life, and so there is no reason to cling to The Only Thing There Is. Endless suffering at the conclusion of one's time in a particular physical form will no longer be demanded or required as a matter of spiritual integrity, any more than it's required of other life forms. This does not mean that ending one's own life as a means of escape from particular difficulties or sadnesses will be or is encouraged. It will be understood that life in one's present physical form is a wondrous gift, and no one will ever wish to toss it away in order to sidestep its challenges, but will understand at the deepest level that it may be used in order to experience who we really are.

In this and in many other ways personal lives will be remarkably different when humans create a new spirituality.

Imagine personal relationships with all others that are no longer need-based, but emerge more profoundly from an experience of personal fulfillment, personal power, and the personal expression of the highest thought about yourself and others that resides within everyone!

Imagine romance that exudes not from the thought that you "can't live without" someone, but from the awareness that the expression and experience of your fullest and highest and grandest Self is not dependent on any other person, but enriches every person whose life you touch immensely, allowing you to truly love from a place of giving!

Imagine a career and work that feels more like joy and the celebration of the highest and best within you, and the happiest experience of Who You Are!

Imagine a life without fear of God and without guilt over the tiniest infraction of what you imagine to be God's Rules!

Imagine the freedom of soul and mind and body that would be experienced when you understand at last that you really *are* One with God! Imagine the power that you would experience—the power to create the life of your dreams, and to assist others in creating theirs!

Imagine the end to frustrations and anxieties and worries about tomorrow, to say nothing of the sadness and bad feelings that can't seem to be shaken about things that happened yesterday, when you realize that *nothing can go wrong*, that all things are perfect just as they are, that God does not require anything different from you except exactly what you are being, exactly what you are doing, and exactly what you are having right now!

Finally, imagine experiencing the awe and wonder of life, expressing through you AS you in your day-to-day moments, because of your wonderfully expanded awareness.

This is just a taste of what life could be like in the days of the New Spirituality, and you don't have to wait for all of humanity to create that experience collectively. All people can begin to create it individually for themselves, and in the lives of those whose lives they touch. That is, in fact, what life invites you to do! It's what God is *calling* you to do right now.

The question now is,
how to use God?

24.

As all of us prepare to do what we are called to do, as we decide *whether to decide* who we are in relationship to each other, in relationship to life, and in relationship to God, it would benefit us to do more of what we have been doing here, in this book. Each day we can look objectively at any beliefs about God and about Life that are coming up for us to see if there may be any that are not working, that are no longer functional.

This means taking a really close look at each area of our lives, just as we have done here, and noticing what we are telling each other about it, and what *we* are being told about it by those we hold as authorities in our lives.

Attention must be paid.

Here is an example of the kind of continuing self-exploration we're talking about. Let's say you're seriously considering marrying, or a friend of yours is, or your child is. Marriage is now on your mind. This is a wonderful time to ask yourself: Are there any other beliefs, besides those that we've already examined here, which cloud your knowing about the truth surrounding marriage?

We talked about marriage before, but let's take a second look, just for a moment. Let's make a closer examination of our culture's "stories" around all this. Let's explore what one of humanity's authoritative sources, the Holy Bible, tells us about marriage.

1. It is acceptable for marriage to consist of a union between one man and one or more women.
    (II Sam. 3:2–5)
2. Marriage does not impede a man's right to take concubines, in addition to his wife or wives.
    (II Sam. 5:13; I Kings 11:3; II Chron. 11:21)
3. A marriage is considered valid only if the wife is a virgin. If the wife is discovered not to be a virgin, the marriage is considered dissolved and the woman is to be executed.
    (Deut. 22:13–21)
4. The marriage of a believer and a nonbeliever is forbidden.
    (Gen. 24:3; Num. 25:1–9; Ezra 9:12; Neh. 10:30)
5. If a married man dies without children, his brother is to marry the widow. If he refuses to marry his brother's widow or deliberately does not give her children, he is to pay a fine of one

shoe, and be otherwise punished in a manner to be determined by law.
(*Gen. 38:6–10; Deut. 25:5–10*)

Of course, no one seriously suggests that the Bible is to be taken literally. It is understood that these and other passages—from all sources and on many topics—simply provide historical context within which larger, timeless messages may be held.

And that is precisely the point.

History is history, but if we try to apply our history literally to our present time, we can do naught but repeat it. And that is not something that I think many of us want to do.

If, as you review some of humanity's collective past, you have the courage to acknowledge that some of our historical ideas about God and about Life are no longer working, then the door is open for you to consider some new ideas to replace them. That first step is the key here. We simply must acquire *a willingness to admit that some of our ideas about God and about Life are no longer working.*

Be kind to yourself as you approach this, understanding that in evolutionary terms we humans are indeed children, and so we can be forgiven for our stubbornness and our inability to see and understand certain things—much less admit them.

A lot of people like to think of humans as a highly evolved species. In fact, humanity has just emerged from its *infancy* on this planet. In their book *New World New Mind,* Robert Ornstein and Paul Ehrlich place this into astonishing perspective in one mind-boggling paragraph:

Suppose Earth's history were charted on a single year's calendar, with midnight January 1 representing the origin of the Earth and midnight December 31 the present. Then each day of Earth's "year" would represent 12 million years of actual history. On that scale, the first form of life, a simple bacterium, would arise sometime in February. More complex life-forms, however, come much later; the first fishes appear around November 20. The dinosaurs arrive around December 10 and disappear on Christmas Day. The first of our ancestors recognizable as human would not show up until the *afternoon of December 31. Homo sapiens*—our species—would emerge at around 11:45 P.M. All that has happened in recorded history would occur in the final *minute* of the year.

We see, then, where we are on the scale of things. In their book, Ornstein and Ehrlich make a powerful case that the human species is so primitive that our brains have not yet developed sufficiently to effectively process the data with which we are being presented on a daily basis by life itself.

Could that include the data that we are being presented about *God*?

Of course it could, and it does.

Yet this is not bad news, but good, for while it dramatically illustrates where we are now, it also shows us where we are capable of going. If it gives us reason to understand *how* we have become *what* we have become, it gives us equal reason to now see clearly how we *can* become what we *choose* to become.

We are in the most exciting time ever to be alive. On the Ornstein-Ehrlich scale, humanity is about to enter Minute Two. I believe that we're preparing now to abandon the stale scenario—lived out at least once before—in which our technology exceeds our ability to spiritually deal with it, to abandon our reptilian fight-or-flight response to nearly every threatening situation, to abandon our insistence on Separation Theology as the final word on How Things Are in the universe, and to expand our awareness to include possibilities never before embodied in the human experience.

I believe we are ready to prove Shakespeare right.

"There are more things in heaven and earth . . . ," he wrote, "than are dreamt of in your philosophy."

25.

There is a final topic to be addressed here, and it is by far the most exciting. It is about *how* to create life as we would like to experience it on this planet.

Earlier, two Basic Questions of Theology were explored.

The two questions were:

1. Who and What is God?
2. What does God want, and why?

The answers to those questions were:

1. God is life, and everything in life.
2. God wants nothing, because God has, and *is,* everything that God could possibly want.

Now if those answers are correct, a third question logically follows:

3. Then what is God's purpose, what is God's function?

This might be put more bluntly as: <u>What's the point of having a God?</u>

It's one thing to say that there is no separation at all, that "separation" as an *aspect of life* simply does not exist, that all things in life are combined, coagulated, co-joined, connected—that the Creator and the Created are One. But so what? Is that IT? God and we are One? That's the New Spirituality?

No. There's more to it than that. There's more to it than the fact that God is everything.

<u>God can be *used*.</u>

<u>THAT is the point of having a God.</u>

Earlier I said that there is a good reason for believing in God. I also said that *this is the reason*. The force, the power, the energy, that is life itself can be *used,* with consistent and predictable results. Interestingly, this point is made over and over again in the teachings of all religions.

All religions have taught that God's power can be used. Most, however, have taught humans to reach outside themselves to access that power. The New Spirituality will invite humans to go *within*. The new teaching will be:

IF YOU DO NOT GO WITHIN
YOU GO WITHOUT

Social scientist and anthropologist Jean Houston puts it far more eloquently in her book, *Jump Time*. Says she, "People are like stained-glass windows. They sparkle and shine, but when darkness sets in, their true beauty is revealed only if there is light from within." Gods light

This idea has already seeped into humanity's common culture. It was perhaps most memorably expressed for the younger generation in the one-sentence utterance of a filmmaker's futuristic master:

"The Force is with you."

The question now is, how to use God?

It's simple. Thought, word, and deed.

What you think, what you say, and what you do is how you use God.

These are the three Tools of Creation, and the tools are perfect. They are magnificent. They are effective.

Think only what you choose to experience, say only what you choose to make real, do only what you choose to demonstrate as your Highest Reality.

Look at this closely. Is this not what every master has done? Has any master done more?

Nope.

In a word, nope.

But now here is another secret. When you desire something, look to see what *feeling* you imagine you would experience if you had that. Why? Because—and this is an enormous clue—it's always an *internal* experience that your soul is seeking, not an external experience. Most people think that what they want is something on the outside. It is not. It's something on the inside. It is this for which all of humanity is searching, and "feeling" is the word we have given to this experience.

This is the most liberating insight of personal growth work, because it means that *nothing exterior to yourself is required at any time* for you to know inner peace and inner joy.

This is exactly what God knows in every moment. This is what God IS. And that is why it's possible to say, categorically, that *What God Wants* from humanity is nothing at all.

You'll want nothing at all as well when you realize that it is *feelings* that you are after, that these are all you have ever been after, and that any of these that you wish to experience are available within you at any moment.

Feelings are the language of the soul. It's through feelings that the soul speaks to the mind of who you are, and of your connection to All That Is. Throughout your life you are seeking to feel how you felt before you separated from All That Is. This is the yearning that you have not been able to identify, but which you have always known. This is the impulse of life itself.

It is through feelings that all external events are experienced. This is not true of lower forms of life. Ken Keyes Jr. makes this point in another of his books, *Your Roadmap to Lifelong Happiness.* If a snake bites you, Ken tells us, that does not mean it is angry. Snakes don't know about anger. They have no such feelings. They act on instinct, instructed by a limited reptilian brain to act in accordance with survival needs given certain exterior stimuli. A snake cannot respond to *interior* stimuli. It has none.

A mammal, on the other hand, has both. The mammalian brain developed after the reptilian brain as life forms continued to evolve upon the earth. It is the second level of brain matter, and it is where *feelings* are experienced. A lion can become angry if his territory is challenged. A lion acts in accordance with survival needs, given certain exterior *and* interior stimuli.

A human being has yet a third level of brain development. The human brain is where thinking, logic, and reasoning occurs. It is where the data from both the sensing and the feeling processors (the reptilian and the mammalian brains) is put together, analyzed, and understood at a higher level. It is where *conscious decisions* are made, based on all the input. The difference between conscious decisions and unconscious decisions is that *consciousness considers consequences.*

When human beings act without thinking about the outcome of their actions, they are said to be "acting like animals." We *are* animals, of course. We are mammals, and we have mammalian brains, built upon reptilian brains. We have the same fight-or-flight response mechanisms as snakes. We have the same anger as lions. And we have the reasoning capabilities of higher life forms, of highly evolved beings. But of course we must use them. And feelings are a great tool of the brain that most people are not using in their most effective way. *Most people spend their lives reacting to feelings rather than creating with them.*

So now, before we part company, I want to share with you this extraordinary information. This directly answers the question, "If God wants nothing, then what is the point of having a God?"

The point of having a God is to *use* the essence and the energy that IS God, and that is *life,* in a way that allows you to create your own experience, thereby becoming as God is: the creator.

← New Age talk.

26

Because of the way God made you (that is, because of the way God Is), any feeling can be experienced without a stimulating corollary external event. This is without a doubt one of the greatest secrets of life. This is *how God works.*

Did you know that you can simply *think* of an event and capture the feeling you wish to experience?

Watch a scary movie sometime—or a romantic one. You don't actually have to move through an external experience with your body to have all the feelings that a person who is moving through it is having. You can even know that the person you are watching on the screen is *not* moving through it, but is simply *acting.* It makes no difference. You can have a feeling anyway. Movie producers call this "suspending disbelief." Their job is to make a movie so realistic that you literally stop the stopping of your believing.

You can use the same technology on the movie screen

of your mind, placing yourself in the starring role and calling *action!* You may have any feeling you desire at any moment you wish. And now, here's the real miracle. Often you'll find that creating a feeling inside you can create an event outside you.

Did you hear that? That is not a small statement there! That is an enormous announcement. *Creating a feeling inside you can create an event outside you.* This is because feelings move energy around, and energy is the stuff of life.

This phenomenon is discussed with extraordinary insight in the classic book *The Power of Positive Thinking,* written over fifty years ago by the Reverend Dr. Norman Vincent Peale, a Christian minister who understood that feelings are a gift from God, giving us the power of creation. That book has sold millions of copies and is still easy to find today, in libraries, in bookstores, and from any online bookseller.

A more updated and non-Christian-oriented look at this amazing process is offered in the contemporary book *Ask and It Is Given,* by Esther and Jerry Hicks, which speaks about the power of joy—how to get in touch with it, how to create it, and how to use it as a magnificent device with which to produce experiences rich and full.

The fact that you can create something by picturing it in your mind, by *seeing it* as already accomplished, and by allowing yourself to experience the *feeling* associated with that is evidence of the greatest news humanity has ever heard: God wants nothing.

If God wanted something specific from us, God would hardly give us the power to create anything *we* want! And yet we have this power. Do you believe this? If you do not believe it, then, of course, you do not have the power—because you are *using the power to create the reality that you do not have it.*

("As you believe, so will it be done unto you.")

God says only one thing to humanity: "My will for you is your will for you." This opens up the space for miracles. *Personal* miracles, in your own daily life.

This is how God cares for you. God cares for you by giving you the power to care for yourself. Each human being has the ability to create his or her reality. All human beings are creators, and we are creating our reality in every single moment of now. That is why Now is the most important moment there is—a point made eloquently by Eckhart Tolle in his own extraordinary book *The Power of Now.*

And it is not what you *do* in the moment of Now that is the most important element of the creative process, it is how you *feel.* Your feelings create your inner reality, and your inner reality creates your outer experience.

This puts you squarely in the driver's seat. Unfortunately, many people don't know how to drive. They are out of control, because feelings can so often "come over them" out of nowhere, and run them. Often, what they have done in such moments has affected their entire lives.

I hear this so often in the ReCreating Yourself retreats that I present around the world. In these intensive retreats I tell participants, "You may have any feeling you desire. Feelings can be Things Chosen, they do not have to be Things Endured."

Feelings are created by thoughts, I tell them, and every thought is nothing more than an idea conjured up in your mind *that is not reality, but is merely an idea—your idea— ABOUT reality.*

Part of what we do in the ReCreating Yourself retreats is invite people to give up their "story." A story, in my vocabulary, is a top-to-bottom, start-to-finish scenario that we create in our minds about someone or something based on an Originating Thought that popped into our minds, usually given birth by a judgment.

Once you understand this, you can literally decide to feel any way you wish about any experience you are having—and in that moment experience it in a new way if you choose. You can even decide *ahead of time* how you are going to feel under certain conditions or circumstances.

There is the story of a man who, driving down a country road late one night, had a flat tire. Opening his trunk, he discovered that he was without a jack. He immediately looked around. "Perhaps I can find someone nearby who will lend me a jack," he thought, and started down the road. But then he began creating his own story about everything as he walked.

"I'm in the middle of the country," he cried. "There won't be a house for miles." But then he saw a farmhouse just ahead. "It's so late," he said to himself. "There's probably no one up." Then he saw a light in the window. "It's probably just a night-light," the man told himself. "The whole family is fast asleep, and the farmer will have worked all day in the fields and be impossible to wake up and I'll have to bang on the door and bang on the door forever until someone comes, and if the farmer does wake up he's going to be furious with me for getting him out of bed, and when I tell him I need a jack he's going to say, 'My God, man, I have to get dressed and go all the way down to the barn to get one!' and he's going to be really angry now and probably slam the door right in my face, and, and . . ."

By this time the man had arrived at the farmhouse door, agitated beyond all measure. He banged on the door especially hard—and the door swung open almost at once. "Yes?" said the startled farmer inside. "What do you mean, acting like that?" the man blurted. "What kind of a person are you? Can't you see I'm in trouble here? All I want is a simple favor! All I need is a jack! Now don't even *think* about slamming that door on me!"

At which point the farmer slammed the door.

There is scarcely a human being alive who hasn't had at least some version of this happen in his or her life. This is a little-understood experience, even though it is created by one of the most powerful life tools ever used by humans. Most humans use it unwittingly.

This process of deciding our feelings ahead of time can be used in a positive way or in a negative way, and regrettably, it is most often used by people in a negative way—usually because, I'll say again, people do not know they are using it, and would, in fact, *deny* using it. This advance thought about something, given birth by a judgment before the fact, is called a pre-judgment, or *prejudice*.

One can have healthy prejudices, and one can have unhealthy prejudices. Unhealthy prejudices are judgments that you make ahead of time that bring you stress or produce some negativity, such as anger, resentment, or fear. Healthy prejudices are judgments made ahead of time that bring you positive experiences of inner peace, inner joy, or well-being.

You can look at the anticipated events in your life (far more of them are easily predictable than you might at first imagine), and you can decide *before these incidents occur* how you are going to feel about them. This may seem "calculating," and it is! There is nothing "wrong" with being calculating, especially when you are devising the best emotional outcome for you and all concerned. This is what I call Positive Prejudice. You can also create a new perception about what is going on right here, right now.

Byron Katie, the creator of a process that she calls the Work, speaks with marvelous clarity about all this in *Loving What Is*, written with Stephen Mitchell. The Work is very similar to the What's So Process that I use in the ReCreating Yourself retreats. Both processes invite people to look at their thought about something versus their actual experience. That is, their "story" versus their on-the-ground, in-the-moment reality.

When people are willing to give up their "story," their perception changes and amazing things happen. And when people are willing to give up their "story" about *What God Wants,* entire lives can be changed.

27.

There is very little in life that you are experiencing for the first time. Fear is not a first-time experience for anyone. Nor is anger. Nor is love. You have experienced all before.

By this time in your life, in fact, it may be true to say that you are incapable of having any new emotional experience, for the simple reason that there are none. All that is new are the *exterior conditions or circumstances* that create or stimulate the emotional experience you are having. Yet even these are not very new. They are usually simply variations on a theme. They are trigger mechanisms that remind you of a previous physical experience and invite you to react emotionally. That is, they invite you to, quite literally, re-*act*, or *act again,* as you did before.

This is what happens when we use our lower brain—the combination of the reptilian brain and the mammalian brain that I spoke of earlier.

This part of our brain cannot and does not differentiate. It *does not know the difference* between things. It cannot tell time. It cannot separate any one moment from another moment, nor any one person from another person. It thinks that yesterday is now and now is yesterday, seeing them both as one. It could, for instance, think that your spouse is your parent, seeing them both as one.

One of your parents may have said something to you as a child that hurt you very much, because she was the person from whom you most sought approval, and now, today, when your spouse says the same thing or the same kind of thing, *your lower brain thinks it is your parent talking.*

And, because your emotions have been held back for so long, your reaction may be way out of proportion to the "offense" that occurred. Only when things have calmed down a bit will both you and your spouse wonder where in the world all that anger or resentment came from.

They came from the invitation of your mind to think that *now* is *before,* that *here* is *there,* and that *they* are *them.* Our fight-or-flight mechanism is turned on. It's "self-survival time."

Masters refuse this invitation. They see everything *as if it were* for the first time, as if nothing like it had ever happened before. They look deeply into what is being felt and explore the truth about it. Masters come to each moment with original thinking, rather than original sin.

In this way, masters see the Present Moment—that is, what is happening here and now—rather than seeing the re-creation of some previously experienced moment, and the story that has been built up around it. Thus, what for others would have been a time of reaction becomes for the master a time of creation.

It can be the same with you. You can consciously choose how to feel. You can do this by allowing your feelings to be determined by your higher brain, not your reptilian and mammalian brains, your lower brain. You can quite literally *raise your consciousness.* In that moment your feelings, like those of the master, also become creations and not reactions. They become your best friends.

Even those feelings that you do not consciously choose can be your friends, because they signal to you how much distance there is between your inner truth and your outer reality.

In *Loving What Is* Byron Katie writes, "It is easy to be swept away by some overwhelming feeling, so it's helpful to remember that any stressful feeling is like a compassionate alarm clock that says, 'You're caught in the dream.' Depression, pain, and fear are gifts that say, 'Sweetheart,

take a look at what you're thinking right now. You're living in a story that isn't true for you.' "

The moment you experience a negative feeling, you
can say to your subconscious, "Thank you for showing me
that," then release and let go of that negativity before you
make it true, and before it turns into an emotion.

Emotion is energy in motion (e + motion). It is what
you *do* with the feelings you *have*. A feeling is simply a
thought that you hold about something. An emotion is an
eruption, an emergence, an expressing of that thought in
a particular way. It *makes that thought real* by putting it into
action. It is an out-picturing of an inner idea.

Often we "display our emotions." That is, the body
does stuff (we jump for joy!) that telegraphs to the world
what we are feeling. There's a very soft difference here, I
know. To me it seems that an "emotion" is what our mind
tells the body to do about what we feel. We "feel" a thing,
and then get "all emotional." That is, full of Energy in
Motion.

Feelings are always true. Emotions can sometimes be
deceiving. A person standing across the street, watching
another person cry, has no idea what's going on. He does
not know what the second person is feeling, only that the
second person is being very emotional about it. The feeling could be sadness—or great happiness.

So feelings are our deepest truth. Emotions are the

mental and physical manifestations of feelings after the mind gets through with its endless (and rapid) analysis of them.

The mind doesn't know a darn thing about feelings. Only the heart does. The mind *thinks* it knows, of course, and so comes up with all sorts of responses. Some of them are actually in harmony with our true feelings. Some are not.

At moments of great decision and choice in our lives, it would benefit us to therefore go deep inside and look at our True Feelings. Therein is our truth—not in our Emotions.

The What's So Process that I use in the ReCreating Yourself retreats is a wonderful way to do this with a particular issue or an immediate problem. The great thing about this process is that once you learn how to use it, you can run through it at home. You can use it any time, any place, you wish. You may want to do it with paper and pencil at first, but after you use it a number of times, it'll become automatic. It's really a mental process that you can go over in your mind very quickly, without anyone knowing that you're doing it.

This gives you a second level of mastery in creating your day-to-day, moment-to-moment experience. The first level of mastery is to consciously decide how you *choose to feel* about a certain thing. The second level of mastery is to consciously decide how you choose to *express* any feeling you are having, whether you chose that feeling deliberately or not. These are the aims of the What's So Process.

This is powerful stuff. This two-layer mechanism is the Tool of Tools.

Negativity does not have to be that which overcomes you; negativity can be that which you overcome.

28.

When we let go of our "story" about *What God Wants,* we can let go at last of two feelings that we never again have to experience or choose: fear and guilt. I have said that fear and guilt are the only enemies of humanity. This is profoundly true.

Guilt is pointless, and it is not the same as regret. Regret is the feeling that tells us we are sorry for what we did and do not wish to do it again. Guilt is the feeling that *indicts us for it,* and never lets us redeem ourselves no matter *what* we do. Regret is empowering, guilt is paralyzing.

Fear is pointless, and it is not the same as caution. Caution is the feeling that tells us we would benefit from looking both ways before stepping off the curb. Fear is the feeling that won't let us step off the curb at all. Caution is empowering, fear is paralyzing.

Fear is a feeling that, like all feelings, creates vibrations. Earlier we learned that feelings can produce the apparency of reality. This is because feelings move energy around, feelings are energy, and energy is the stuff of life. Fear itself is an energy, a vibration.

Everything is a vibration. Quantum physics and super-string theory—and now the latest articulation of this, called M-theory—tell us that everything in existence is composed not of points, or "dots," of energy, but of smaller-than-minuscule circular "strings" that vibrate constantly, at differing rates. These strings have the ability to interconnect, or intertwine, with each other, creating a "superstring."

Is it possible that "superstring" vibrations can be created with the mind? When we walk into a room where people have been having an argument, even though the argument may have stopped the moment we entered, we know we have walked into a room with *bad vibes.* We can feel it. Did those arguing people create those vibes?

Feelings can be felt *in the air.* And the more compact the space, the easier it can be to feel this. That's because the feeling—that is, the *energy*—is concentrated in one space, and the fewer the people, the fewer will be the variations in the mix, making energy less diluted and much easier to identify.

All of us create variations in the energy flow around us. We produce fluctuations. We, *ourselves,* are fluctuations. We are ever-changing alterations in the energy field that swirls about us. Our fluctuations in turn create other fluctuations, or "disturbances," in the energy field adjacent to our energy field, and those affect the field around that, and those around that, and so on—outward and ever outward in an eternal distribution of energy that touches bigger and bigger fields of influence the farther it radiates from the originating Source, but with smaller and smaller impact the greater the distance from that Source.

In this way every thought affects the whole world— indeed, to some degree, the universe. How much? Probably not very significantly, given the lack of pure focus and consistency in the energy that most people emanate. Yet if that energy is focused and consistent, if it becomes a pinpoint of laser sharp and unremitting clarity, it can cut through virtually any obstacle in the surrounding energy field, reshaping that field in the form that we, as individuals, choose.

It is in this way that many people have learned to deeply affect and dramatically impact their personal reality. They *live the lives they choose.* And when many individuals make the same choice *collectively,* the *combined* energy of *collective consciousness* can have an immediate and detectable influence on the larger reality in any environment. Ultimately, this can affect life on earth itself.

So the trick here is focus and consistency, the fuel here is feeling, and the tool is thought. How do we focus?

How do we maintain consistency? Here, too, we have been given an easy-to-understand, easy-to-use mechanism. That mechanism is Intention.

We are affecting our creative energy with our intentions in every moment. We either do this consciously or unconsciously, but we do it all the time. To the degree to which our intentions are clear to us, to that degree we become consciously creative. To the degree to which our own intentions arise from a sub-agenda that even we are not aware of (a subconscious reaction), to that degree our energy becomes scattered, and we find it very difficult to produce any particular or desired result in our lives.

Life proceeds out of your intentions for it.

This has been said before, many times. You are invited in this moment to pay attention to it. *Pay attention to your intention.* And let go of guilt and fear as your first step in moving to clarity about your intentions, for guilt and fear only cloud them.

29.

There is one thing you will notice in all of this discussion about *What God Wants* and about the process of life and pure creation. You are at the center of all of it.

There has been only one thing missing from your understanding of God.

You.

You have been what's missing.

But you're not missing anymore.

Once you were lost, but now you are found. You have found yourself in God. And you have found God, in yourself.

God is One Being, or, seen in another way, God is One, *Being*.

And what is God Being? God is Being what God Is.

Think on this.

Ponder these things deeply in your heart.

Now understanding expands. Suddenly it's clear that what God is BEING is what God Is. The "being" and the "isness" are the same. God is *being* what God *is*, and God *is* what God is *being*. It's a circle. There is no beginning and no end to this. Do not look for a beginning and an end, because you'll search in vain for That Which Is Not. There is only That Which Is. There is only One God. What God is this? Is it Adonai? Allah? Elohim? God? Hari? Jehovah? Krishna? Lord? Rama? Vishnu? Yahweh?

It's All of Them.

Now the words start whittling away. Words are the least reliable form of communication. As the search for higher meaning advances, words do their best job by falling away.

God is being what God is.

God is being what God?

God is being what?

God is being.

God is.

God.

30.

God is God. Or, to use God's own words:

I AM THAT I AM.

I heard this so often during my growing-up years.

I am that I am, sayeth the Lord.

I never knew what that meant. Then one day, years later, I was walking down a street with a master teacher of mine. I saw a man lying up against a building, dirty, smelly, unshaven, holding an empty bottle of wine in a limp hand. He was snoring. "There, but for the grace of God, go I," I whispered. My teacher looked at me and said, "No. There, *because* of the grace of God, you go."

I didn't understand, and so my teacher explained.

"Every time you see something outside yourself, don't separate yourself from it, merge with it. Become one with it. You are one with everything. Don't encourage yourself in thinking thoughts of separation. Look at that man and say, 'There I am, being a drunk.' Look at the movie star and say, 'There I am, being famous.' Look at the grass and say, 'There I am, being the grass.' Just keep seeing yourself everywhere. Just look and say, 'I am that.' Practice this daily and it will give you, in three months, an entirely different outlook on life."

And so I did. I walked around saying this in my head. I would glance at something and tell myself, "I am that." One day I was explaining to someone who was taking a walk with me why I was looking at things in such a deep way. Apparently I had some sort of expression on my face that gave it away. I was asked, "What are you thinking?" And I said, "Well, actually, I was thinking that I am that."

"You are that? What are you talking about?"

And so I started pointing to things all around me, saying, "I am that, I am that, I am that . . ." And my friend interrupted me. "No, you're not. You're you." And I replied, "Not really. Not in ultimate reality. In the world of our illusion I am 'me,' over here, but in ultimate reality I am 'me' over here, and I am that."

My friend shot me a quizzical look.

I said, "No, really. I am that . . . *I am.*"

Then a chill went up my back. I suddenly imagined God walking around, pointing to things, saying to an unbelieving world, "I am that, *I am.*"

In that moment I was set free.

And now you are free.

Free of any limiting thoughts you ever had about

yourself. Free of any idea you may still have been holding on to that God and you are separate from each other.

And all the world's souls can be set free. The New Spirituality is a civil rights movement for the soul, freeing humanity at last from the oppression of its belief in a separate, angry, violent, and fearful God.

Human beings have always *been* free. They simply have not known it.

Neither you, nor any of your ancestors, nor your ancestors' ancestors, have ever failed God. You have never disobeyed God, because God has never issued you any orders. Whom would God command? And to whom would God mete out punishment were His commands not kept? Would God use His right hand to slap His left?

A New Spirituality truly is emerging upon the earth, and the idea of Oneness is at its core. This reality gives birth to the concept of Non-Neediness. Divinity is seen as being Whole and Complete, wanting and needing nothing.

This New Spirituality, to make it clear once again, seeks not to replace the present religions of humanity but to expand them, not to remove them but to refresh them, not to reject them but to reinvigorate them with larger truth and greater relevance for a New Millennium.

There is nothing sacrilegious about this New Spirituality; neither is it apostasy, blasphemy, or heresy. It is, however, different. Vastly different from what has been taught thus far in the world's mainstream religions. And for this very reason, it can be of enormous value to humanity.

It's the same old stories about God and about Life that are killing you. The same old thoughts, the same old words, the same old deeds.

So here is the New Spirituality in three words:

God is everything.

What a profound revelation! What a remarkable insight! What a life-changing awareness!

Out of this awareness flows a flawless sequitur:

God wants nothing.

Immediately you begin to understand. At once, you begin to see. You have been blind, but now you see.

We human beings do not need to be saved from the "snares of the Devil," we need to be saved from ourselves. We are threatening to condemn ourselves to Hell right here on the earth. We can yet create Heaven on earth, but we must choose now very wisely.

We must choose between ancient myths, age-old cultural stories, and outdated theologies, or new truths, greater wisdoms, and grander visions of a God and a World united, expressing as One, projecting the glory of Life Itself *into* life itself, and producing the possibility, at last, of a New Way of Life for All Humanity.

We must choose between Yesterday and Tomorrow.

Humanity is being given an invitation to explore the wondrous possibilities of Tomorrow's God, and the world that this new God can create.

It's not a new God at all, of course, only a new understanding of the present God, of the one God, of The Only Thing That Is.

That new understanding can launch the Thousand Years of Peace of which it has been written. It can give birth to a Golden Age of Glory.

31.

Very few people will be able to believe what's in this book.

At least, at first.

There will come a day when everyone will accept what has been said here as an "of course." On that future date all of this will seem so *obvious*. Even today it is obvious to some. There are those who *will* believe the message here right now, this moment. Of these, a few will find it difficult to sit still. They'll want to do something with what they've heard, because they'll recognize immediately that it can change everything in our world.

These will be the fearless ones, stepping into uncharted territory, blazing a trail for those who would follow, dreaming the dreams that only the courageous can dream.

They may not hold positions of great visibility, but they'll soon be seen as candles that truly light the world.

They may not be found in places of great power, but they'll soon empower an entire species to claim its inheritance and live out its destiny at last. They will, therefore, be among those human beings who change life on the earth in remarkable ways. And this will be their legacy.

You may be one of this select few. If your soul leaps with joy at the message revealed here in such simple terms that it can no longer be misunderstood, distorted, or denied, you are. If your mind races with new possibilities for your own life and for people everywhere as a result of that message, you are.

If you are, you may find yourself beginning to live the messages that you have found here. And by your living of them, you will be silently inviting others to consider the dramatically alternative ideas that inform your experience, for others will not be able to ignore your behavior, and they will wonder what you know and how you have come to know it.

That will be the perfect time for you to extend what I call the Quiet Invitation. Your behavior, your life lived, is the first part of your Quiet Invitation. Others around you will soon desire to explore the extraordinary possibilities that your thoughts present. When they ask you how it can be that you move through the world so much of the time with such peace and joy and love, you will tell them. Quietly, without any attempt at "converting" or proselytizing, you will simply tell them what you understand of the world, of life, and of God.

You'll do this because you know that these ideas could turn your world upside down—and because you see that your world could use a little upside-down-turning right now. And you'll do it because you know that if someone like you does *not* do it, no one else will.

It's true that the message presented here will come to the attention of many persons in positions of influence and visibility. It is too astonishing a message not to make its way to people of high profile within government, business, media, entertainment, sports, academia, and religion. It is also true that, of these, a handful may find that they actually agree with the message. Hardly any, however, will be able to admit it.

Prominent people of influence and power do not like to make too many other people uneasy. That's the problem with prominence. If you are married to your prominence, you are often divorced from your power. Prominent people cannot, therefore, be expected to do much in a public way to activate the ideas with which they may agree if those ideas are unconventional. Some do. Most do not.

Corruption comes in many forms, including corruption of the conscience, of the mind, and of the will. It's the last of these that is the most devastating.

Most corruption is not placed into the world by what people do, but by what they do not do. To do nothing is to do everything. Saying nothing is saying yes.

No, it turns out, has to be spoken.

Because it's difficult for people in prominent positions to say no to humanity's present ideas about God and about Life, new leadership will have to be found if new ideas are to reach a larger number of people for their consideration and exploration.

The first qualification for becoming one of these new leaders is willpower. Humanity must regain its collective will, and new leaders must show it the way by leading the way.

That's where you come in.

Please consider the possibility that *you brought yourself to this healing message at this moment* in answer to a call from your own soul. It is a call to soar. It is a feeling of yearning from deep within for you to *make a difference* in a world of *in*difference.

Because of that indifference, our world is being taken from us. The life of which we have dreamed is slowly turning into the nightmare of which we have despaired, and it will continue to do so if we do not now wake up.

We have seen the sun set on the hopes of many. Yet, as Ernest Hemingway so eloquently said, the sun also rises. Let us not now sleep through the dawn. This is the time of the awakening of humanity.

Shall we arise, one by one, and gently wake one another?

AFTERWORD

This may very well be one of the most important books you've ever read. That could be true whether you agree with it or disagree with it.

If you disagree with it, I have no doubt that it has made you more clear about your own point of view than ever, and that's a good thing. If you agree with it, I am equally sure that it has been helpful.

May I say, please, that the purpose of this book is not to get you to agree with its contents, but something far more important: _to reopen the discussion about God—about Who God Is and about What God Wants._ If it has done that, and only that, it will have served its purpose.

I want to thank you for your courage in exploring this topic with me. As I know that you know, any new or different thought about God is discouraged by many people. These are people who say they know all there is to know about this. They'll tell you that _the last thing God wants_ is a new thought about _What God Wants._

No new thought allowed. That's the rule. Any movement toward a new thought is demonized. The New Thought Movement is considered the work of Satan. There are those who will tell you that you are risking the salvation of your immortal soul if you are even seriously exploring, to say nothing of embracing, the new thoughts found here.

If humanity had taken the same position with regard to new thoughts in science, technology, or medicine, it would have made virtually no progress in the past 300 years. It's true that even in those fields new ideas were often slow in being accepted, but at least they were allowed. At least they could be *introduced,* and eventually even discussed.

Not so in theology. Serious discussion of any possibility regarding God and life that is not in agreement with the notions commonly accepted within a particular culture is not only discouraged, in some places it is labeled an *offense against the faith* and punishable accordingly. Even in a work of *fiction* differing ideas about the Almighty may not be explored. Remember Salman Rushdie?

In the United States things are a little less confrontational. Stunningly new ideas about God are simply ignored. I've written five *New York Times* best sellers about God, and the *Times* itself has never reviewed a single one.

When it comes to its most sacred beliefs, our society

will not tolerate new ideas that violate doctrine—or even question it. Thus, we are trying to build a twenty-first-century reality with first-century moral, ethical, and spiritual tools. This would be akin to a surgeon stepping into a modern-day operating room with a very sharp stone.

It is not necessary to build our tomorrows with such primitive tools. The prohibition against new ideas and new thoughts about God can and must be lifted. A new discussion about God and about *What God Wants* must begin.

"The age in which we live is shivering amidst the tremors of ontological breakdown," says Jean Houston in her extraordinary book *Life Force*. "It's all shifting: the moral mandates; the structural givens; the standard-brand governments, religions, economics; the very consensual reality is breaking down, the underlying fabric of life and process by which we organized our reality and thought we knew who and why and where we were.

"The world by which we understood ourselves—a world that began in its essential mandates several thousand years ago with certain premises about humanity, God, reality, and the moral and metaphysical order, and which in terms of our existential lives, began about three hundred years ago with the scientific revolution—is a world that no longer works. It is a world whose lease has run out, whose paradigms are eroding, and which no longer provides us with the means and reference points by which we can understand ourselves. We are not unlike the cartoon cat who runs off the cliff and keeps on running, treading air over the abyss before he discovers his predicament and says, 'Oops!'

"There is a lag between the end of an age and the discovery of that end. We are the children of the lag, the people of the time of parenthesis—and there is no juicier time to be alive. For the future is open in a time of parenthesis—the new age is being seeded; the new myths are beginning to appear. . . ."

You can help in that process. I know that many of you want to. There is one question that I have been asked more than any other during the years since the publication of my first book. People who have been profoundly impressed and deeply touched by the liberating freshness of its message have written me by the thousands (over 60,000 letters and e-mails at last estimate) asking, "What can I do to help get this message *out there,* to send this message further, to share and spread these ideas? If these wonderful messages of God's unconditional love can affect others the way they have affected me, I just know they can change the world. How can I at least get people talking about them?"

It will please you to know that people *are* talking about them. The book you are holding in your hand will be read around the world. So we have a jump here. There is much to do, but we are not exactly starting from scratch. We have a wonderful opportunity here. Humanity has a wonderful opportunity.

Our opportunity now is to create the space of possibility for a New Spirituality to emerge upon the earth, a kind of spirituality that will not in any way hinder or destroy our traditional faith traditions, but that will reinvigorate them, refresh them, enliven them, *expand* them, and allow them to flourish, bringing to our world at last an individualized experience of the Divine in a unified form that makes no one wrong for the way in which they are approaching the God of their understanding, and that creates no condemnation or conflict in God's name.

Is this too much to ask of religion?

Is it?

I don't think so. But I know that this kind of healed spirituality cannot fully emerge on the earth without you. For you must be the creators and the carriers of its message. Is this too big a task for you? No. There is much you can do, first, in your own home, in the teaching of your children, in the interactions with your family. Then, in the places that you touch every day. The office. The store. The bank. The mall. The Internet. Bring your energy, bring your changed energy, to those places. Touch the people in those places with that which has touched you—

the wonder and the joy of God's true love, of God's absolute acceptance, of God's comforting and strengthening and empowering presence. *Be the change you wish to see in the world.* Gandhi's extraordinary words cannot be repeated too often.

This business of being the change is easier than you think—and more impacting than you could imagine. It can change everything. For you. For those around you. For those around them. For those around those around them. And on and on and on.

Truly.

Truly.

Believe it.

Now I want to let you know that you need not be alone in this undertaking. That is the wonderful news, and that is the point I hope you will take away from all this. Hundreds, thousands—nay, millions—are thinking now as you are thinking: What can I do? How can I work, in my small way, to heal our world, to make it a better place, to bring an end to this insanity? What can I do to assist all of us to take a look at our beliefs, and to alter those beliefs which lead to our own self-destruction?

And so, you have allies. You have companions. It is as John Kennedy said. Divided, there is little we can do. Together, there is little we cannot do.

Let us, then, work together.

One of the first things we can do is keep abreast of what *others* are doing. That is why I have created *Changing Beliefs: The Newsletter of the New Spirituality,* a publication read by thousands, available online or in your mailbox. It's filled with inspiring stories of how people's lives have been touched by the unconditionally loving God described in this book, how-to articles on applying the principles of the New Spirituality to daily life, and information connecting you to people in your own neighborhood and around the world who are working to place a new thought about God and about Life into the marketplace of ideas, and ultimately, into the human culture.

This wonderful newsletter may be obtained by subscription at newsletter@cwg.org. The link will take you to a sign-up page providing you with a fast and easy way to have this monthly gift for the soul sent winging to you by e-mail. (If you do not use a computer, you may receive the newsletter in your mailbox by writing to the street address found below.)

Another way to move forward in your larger understanding and real-world application of the messages found here is through participation in our ReCreating Yourself retreats, which focus on personal growth and spiritual development. These retreats feature the What's So Process mentioned in the narrative of this book, in which people are given the opportunity to let go of their "story" and move from reaction to creation in the important moments of their lives. For more information about schedule and location, go to www.nealedonaldwalsch.com. You can check out our new "CwG blog" there as well.

Finally, you may wish to apply for enrollment in the Life Education Program (LEP), empowering you to become an effective and confident presenter of New Spirituality lectures, classes, seminars, workshops, or full-scale retreats, or to become a New Spirituality Life Coach and Peer Counselor, helping others on an individual basis to find their true path and highest way.

In all of these activities you'll be giving people back to themselves. That is the mission of a nonprofit organization with which I am associated that seeks to produce a re-created humanity through greater spiritual understanding. It is this foundation that sponsors the newsletter and the LEP you've just heard about, and many other programs and activities offering people an invitation and an opportunity to re-create themselves anew in the next grandest version of the greatest vision they ever held about who they are.

Our foundation consists of a small paid staff, usually around half a dozen, depending upon needs, and a handful of deeply committed volunteers working together to bring the message of the book you are holding, as well as the other books in the series I have written, called *Conver-*

sations with God, to the world at large. We believe it is a message that can bring wonderful healing to our planet.

We hope that you'll feel moved to connect with us. Here is our contact information:

Conversations with God Foundation
PMB #1150
1257 Siskiyou Blvd.
Ashland, Oregon 97520
telephone: 541.482.8806
website: www.cwg.org
e-mail: info@cwg.org

You may also wish to connect simultaneously with our sister organization, Humanity's Team, to which our foundation gave birth, at www.HumanitysTeam.com. Humanity's Team now works collaboratively with us to place New Spirituality study groups, as well as other educational programs and outreach activities, on the ground in cities, towns, and villages around the globe. It is the worldwide embodiment of this effort.

You may also wish to obtain a copy of *Part of the Change: Your Role as a Spiritual Helper,* a short but incisive handbook outlining ten simple steps you can take right now to bring about change in the day-to-day experience of those whose lives you touch. I'll send you an electronic copy by

e-mail, free, if you ask for it. Just go to www.nealedonald
walsch.com and follow the link to the request form.

Finally, you can even join the "bracelets with a message" craze and obtain and give away bracelets that say "I
Am Part of the Change," so that others can know that
you have joined in this worldwide effort. Simply go to
www.partofthechange.com.

On June 23, 2004, a most interesting press release hit
the wire services. A scientific survey conducted by Harris
Interactive the previous month had determined that
69 percent of adult Americans believe *religious differences
are the biggest hurdle to achieving global peace.*

Nothing could be closer to the truth. This is the point
made resoundingly in my two prior books, *The New Revelations* and *Tomorrow's God.* I urge every reader of *What God
Wants* to study those texts for an in-depth look at what is
found on the pages here.

The Harris survey is wonderful news because it shows
that many people are beginning to understand and to acknowledge the true nature of the biggest problem in the
world today. There are many ways to solve this problem,
and Dr. Bruce Chilton, Episcopal priest, author, lecturer,
and professor of theology, believes that one of the most
dynamic approaches might be to challenge the clergy
itself—the people who are carrying the Word of God to

people the world over—to explore more deeply the theological underpinnings of their own understandings.

"As I encounter clergy and scholars of religion, I have become increasingly troubled by how narrow their intellectual formation is," Dr. Chilton told me when I visited with him in the fall of 2004 in his office at Bard College in New York State. "We must act decisively to change that, in my opinion."

I agree. Profoundly. Dr. Chilton told me that he was particularly saddened by his observation that today's theology students don't seem to be asking very many really probing, confrontational, or deeply exploratory questions about the material they're studying. It's almost as if they're reluctant to challenge doctrine at any level—even in theology *school,* where one would think such challenges would be rigorous.

In response to what he was observing, Dr. Chilton founded the Institute for Advanced Theology at Bard.

"The Institute began when local clergy asked me to offer lectures for their continuing education," he told me. That was in 1988, and now it has a diverse membership of spiritually aware, keen, and well-educated friends, ordained and not, from across the spectrum of religious perspectives.

Since 1996 the Institute has also sponsored a series of

conferences, crafted to address issues of comparative theology in historical context. Work arising out of the conferences has all been published and is respected internationally.

But the most exciting initiative, from my perspective, is Dr. Chilton's next goal, which is to put into place *an advanced degree program in comparative theology for current members of the clergy.*

The program, nearly ready for submission to the State of New York for validation at this writing, is designed to broaden the horizon of clergy and scholars of theology, who would also be eligible for admission, and to sensitize them to the mystical traditions of the global religions, Dr. Chilton told me.

"Amidst the signs of religious ill-health that come our way daily," he said, "I can think of no single change that would have as great and immediate an influence on the religious temperament of the United States and the world than broadening the theological horizons of our clergy."

I believe that Bruce Chilton has hit the nail squarely on the head. I observe that he is doing something that is at once courageous and extraordinarily relevant. I am excited by what the Institute that he has founded is doing, and by what it might accomplish in the future.

If what you have learned here about the work of the

Institute of Advanced Theology speaks to you, I hope you will become a part of that work by offering your support. You may do so by sending financial contributions (which are tax deductible) made out to:

> The Institute of Advanced Theology at
> Bard College
> P.O. Box 5000
> Annandale-on-Hudson, NY 12504-5000

The Institute's Internet address is www.bard.edu/iat. You may send an e-mail to: iat@bard.edu. The telephone number is 845.758.7279.

Religion *is* the biggest obstacle to peace in the world today. Let's make no mistake about that. Let's not tiptoe around that fact, either. Let's do as 69 percent of the American people did in the Harris survey. Let's tell it like it is.

This problem has become so pronounced that *New York Times* columnist Nicholas Kristof was moved to write on July 17, 2004:

"If the latest in the *Left Behind* series of evangelical thrillers is to be believed, Jesus will return to Earth, gather non-Christians to his left and toss them into everlasting fire.

"Jesus merely raised one hand a few inches and a yawning chasm opened in the earth, stretching far and wide enough to swallow all of them. They tumbled in, howling and screeching, but their wailing was soon quashed and all was silent when the earth closed itself again.

"These are the best-selling novels for adults in the United States, and they have sold more than 60 million copies worldwide. The latest is *Glorious Appearing*, which has Jesus returning to Earth to wipe all non-Christians from the planet. It's disconcerting to find ethnic cleansing celebrated as the height of piety.

"If a Muslim were to write an Islamic version of *Glorious Appearing* and publish it in Saudi Arabia, jubilantly describing a massacre of millions of non-Muslims by God, we would have a fit. We have quite properly linked the fundamentalist religious tracts of Islam with the intolerance they nurture, and it's time to remove the motes from our own eyes."

Later in the same column Mr. Kristof continues, "This matters in the real world, in the same way that fundamentalist Islamic tracts in Saudi Arabia do. Each form of fundamentalism creates a stark moral division between decent, pious types like oneself—and infidels headed for hell."

Then, echoing some of my own feelings, the *Times* columnist said, "I had reservations about writing this column because I don't want to mock anyone's religious beliefs, and millions of Americans think *Glorious Appearing* describes God's will. Yet ultimately I think it's a mistake to treat religion as a taboo, either in this country or in Saudi Arabia."

Finally, Mr. Kristof used his newspaper opinion piece to ask a piercing question.

"Should we really give intolerance a pass if it's rooted in religious faith?

"Many American Christians once read the Bible to mean that African-Americans were cursed as descendants of Noah's son Ham, and were intended by God to be enslaved. In the 19th century, millions of Americans sincerely accepted this Biblical justification for slavery as God's word—but surely it would have been wrong to defer to such racist nonsense simply because speaking out could have been perceived as denigrating some people's religious faith.

"People have the right to believe in a racist God, or a God who throws millions of nonevangelicals into hell. I don't think we should ban books that say that. But we should be embarrassed when our best-selling books gleefully celebrate religious intolerance and violence against infidels.

"That's not what America stands for, and I doubt that it's what God stands for."

I am certain it's not.

And so we see here, in real-life terms, the nature of

our present dilemma. The question now is not, What is the problem?, but What are we going to do about it?

Whatever we choose to do, we cannot do it alone. It's going to take more than one of us—more, even, than a few of us—to make a difference here. And so, I am embarking now on a daring, and some might say foolhardy, quest. . . .

I know that the *Conversations with God* books have touched millions of people all over the world, changing countless lives for the better. If we could find just a portion of those readers and call upon them to work together now toward the creation of a New Spirituality, we could generate an unstoppable force and an unlimited source of human energy that could turn our world right-side-up at last.

If you resonate with what you've read here, or if you've been touched in a positive way by any of the *Conversations with God* books, please join our global community. Send your e-mail address to: readers@nealedonaldwalsch.com.

You inspire me!

Neale Donald Walsch
January, 2005
Ashland, Oregon

P.S. Of course, the *fastest* thing you can do to move the message of the New Spirituality into the world is to *pass on a copy of this book*. I hope that you'll put it into many hands.

You never change things by
fighting the existing reality.
To change something, build a
new model that makes the
existing model obsolete.
—R. Buckminster Fuller